Praise for
DO THE SHADOW

'Charlie's book on shadow work is a profound exploration of the darker aspects of our psyche – the parts we often avoid but that hold the key to our growth. By bringing our shadow into the light, Charlie shows us how to embrace and work with it, unlocking the personal power that lies within.'
CAGGIE DUNLOP, AUTHOR AND HOST OF THE *SATURN RETURNS* PODCAST

'This is a pioneering resource. Its innovative approach combines Jungian psychology with a spiritual richness that facilitates true personal and psychological growth.'
DR HEATHER SEQUEIRA, CONSULTANT PSYCHOLOGIST AND TRAUMA SPECIALIST

'In the depths of the shadow's darkness lies a treasure beyond price. Charlie's book provides both the compass and the map to that treasure.'
JAMES SCURRY, PSYCHOTHERAPIST AND COFOUNDER OF SAFELY HELD SPACES

'Do the Shadow Work is a powerful invitation to turn inwards and uncover the treasures hidden in the parts of ourselves we often avoid. Charlie Morley's bold, transformative guidance is a gift to anyone ready to step into their wholeness and embrace their light and darkness alike.'
DAVID R. HAMILTON, PHD, AUTHOR OF *THE JOY OF ACTUALLY GIVING A F*CK*

'Life-changing. Charlie offers tried-and-tested methods for retrieving your buried treasure and living a more authentic, joyful and connected life.'
MATTHEW GREEN, AUTHOR OF *AFTERSHOCK: THE UNTOLD STORY OF SURVIVING PEACE*

'Charlie Morley is simply one of the best teachers I know. He combines profound wisdom with wit and humour and turns any topic, even shadow work, into something life changing and so much fun!'

VISHEN LAKHIANI, *NEW YORK TIMES* BESTSELLING AUTHOR OF *THE CODE OF THE EXTRAORDINARY MIND*

'Charlie Morley elegantly dismantles a delicate topic for us all, and offers up a beautiful sigh of relief for those of us embarking on our own journey of self-discovery.'

EDDY ELSEY, AUTHOR OF *LET HEALING HAPPEN*

DO THE
SHADOW
WORK

ALSO BY CHARLIE MORLEY

Books

Dreams of Awakening

Wake Up to Sleep

Lucid Dreaming Made Easy

Dreaming Through Darkness

Guided Meditations
Available on the
Empower You Unlimited Audio
App and Website

Lucid Dreaming Affirmations and Sleep Meditations

Lucid Dreaming Self-Hypnosis

7 Days to Great Sleep Challenge

Lucid Dreaming, Conscious Sleeping

Online Courses

Lucid Dreaming Made Easy

DO THE
SHADOW
WORK

CHARLIE MORLEY

HAY HOUSE

Carlsbad, California • New York City
London • Sydney • New Delhi

Published in the United Kingdom by:
Hay House UK Ltd, 1st Floor, Crawford Corner,
91–93 Baker Street, London W1U 6QQ
Tel: +44 (0)20 3927 7290; www.hayhouse.co.uk

Published in the United States of America by:
Hay House LLC, PO Box 5100, Carlsbad, CA 92018-5100
Tel: (1) 760 431 7695 or (800) 654 5126; www.hayhouse.com

Published in Australia by:
Hay House Australia Publishing Pty Ltd, 18/36 Ralph St, Alexandria NSW 2015
Tel: (61) 2 9669 4299; www.hayhouse.com.au

Published in India by:
Hay House Publishers India, Muskaan Complex, Plot No.3, B-2,
Vasant Kunj, New Delhi 110 070
Tel: (91) 11 4176 1620; www.hayhouse.co.in

A significant part of this book was previously published in 2017 as *Dreaming Through Darkness* (978-1-78180-735-4)

A catalogue record for this book is available from the British Library.

Tradepaper ISBN: 978-1-4019-7964-5
E-book ISBN: 978-1-83782-328-4
Audiobook ISBN: 978-1-83782-327-7

Interior illustrations: 53, 55, 130, 161: Liron Gilenberg (www.ironicitalics.com); 96: Charlie Morley; 122: Dr Garret Yount

10 9 8 7 6 5 4 3 2 1

Printed in the United States of America

This product uses responsibly sourced papers and/or recycled materials. For more information, see www.hayhouse.com.

The authorized representative in the EU for product safety and compliance is Penguin Random House Ireland, Morrison Chambers, 32 Nassau Street, Dublin D02 YH68, Ireland. https://eu-contact.penguin.ie

To Rob Nairn 1939–2023
for lighting my way to the shadow

CONTENTS

Part III: Transforming the Shadow

AUTHOR'S NOTE

This book is an abridged and fully revised version of my 2017 publication, *Dreaming Through Darkness*.

If you are interested in shadow integration within the context of lucid dreaming and Tibetan Buddhism, then the 2017 edition might be even better for you.

But if you're looking for a book that is pure shadow work, full of practical daytime exercises, then the one you have in your hands is exactly what you need.

This new book also includes fully updated exercises, whole new chapters and several brand-new practices that were not in the 2017 edition.

LIST OF EXERCISES

INTRODUCTION

*'Out beyond ideas of wrongdoing
and rightdoing there is a field.
I'll meet you there.'*

RUMI[1]

Almost 20 years ago I was introduced to a practice that changed my life forever. This practice, and the revolutionary perspectives on the mind that it offered, gave me more confidence, more authenticity and access to a vast source of psychological energy, which I found within myself. It was called shadow work.

In the past few years this powerful practice has become popular with the TikTok generation, spawning a whole new movement of people ready to change shame into acceptance and fear into love. In theory, anyway. So much of the shadow work being offered is either so diluted that it doesn't actually lead to any significant shifts or it's so theoretical that you end up saying to yourself, 'Yeah, but how do I actually *do* it?'

This book aims to fill that gap with powerful psychological practices, most of which are science-backed with real-time, real-life results, and all of which are safe to do and have a significantly positive impact on mental wellbeing.

So, what is the shadow exactly? It's the part of us made up of all that we hide from others: our shame, our fears and our wounds, but also our divine spirit, our blinding beauty and our unexpressed talents. There are two aspects of the shadow: dark and golden.

Shadow work involves shining light into the dark caves of our unconscious mind to reveal the gold that is stored there. I believe that we have been looking for that gold in all the wrong places. Our true power is found not in the saccharine sweetness of 'spiritual bypassing' – overlooking our unenlightened human condition – but in the dazzling darkness of our shadow side. The light that we will find there is brighter than we can ever imagine.

In this book we'll use scientifically validated techniques from Western psychology alongside ancient methods from Tibetan Buddhism and Mexican shamanism to power the alchemical process of turning darkness into gold. Every exercise has earned its place in this book and has been developed, tested and refined through the shadow work retreats that I have facilitated in over 20 countries around the world for the past 10 years.

In Part I: Meeting the Shadow, we'll be laying the groundwork and exploring what the shadow is, how it helps to create our emotional baggage and how we project it onto others. We'll use creative writing, guided meditations, drawing and imagination practices to bring us into a direct meeting with our shadow side.

In Part II: Befriending the Shadow, we'll look at shame, trauma, fear and nightmares. We'll also explore the parts of ourselves that we hide from others through a truly powerful exercise called the Two-Faced Mask.

And finally, in Part III: Transforming the Shadow, we'll dive deeper than you may have thought possible as we explore our ancestors, sex and death – where we came from, what made us and what will end us – and transform our shadow into loving awareness, energy and power.

You will be asked to make a pilgrimage back to the lands of your ancestors, heal your relationship with your parents, own your sexual story and face your fear of death. In these last few chapters we'll engage a set of practices that really can change your life.

Dreamwork will be woven in throughout the whole book, not only because this is my other area of expertise but also because our dreams will often reveal changes in our unconscious mind way before our conscious mind notices them.

In writing this book I have set out to reveal the truth of my own shadow too, fully and authentically, as a way of inspiring others to do the same. In using my own stories of shadow integration, I have exposed some of my most seemingly 'shameful' shadow aspects, a few of which may shock some of my more conservative readers. I don't seek to make excuses for these revelations – in fact I believe it is vital that I unmask myself fully if I am to ask you to do the same.

So, be prepared. I will encourage you to move into places that may shock and scare you. You may be shocked by the brilliance of your divine light and scared by the responsibility that comes with this light, for once you have seen how much brilliance you contain, how can you possibly go on living the way you have been?

In fact, this book aims to empower you to change the way you live forever. Just as a single candle can illuminate a cave that has been dark for millennia, so these practices can bring radical illumination to your unseen potential.

Never has there been a better moment to integrate our darkness and own our golden light. The safest and greatest gift we can give the world today is an integrated shadow.

The term 'lightworker' has been used for decades to describe those on the path to self-awakening through love and light. I'm a big fan of love and light, but life isn't always that way, and until we learn to work with the rest of it, we will never be whole. And so I am proud to be part of a new breed of spiritual practitioner. We call ourselves shadow workers. By the end of this book I hope that you will call yourself one too.

The world needs shadow workers now more than ever. So, let us move into the freedom of shamelessness, the place beyond duality, beyond right and wrong, the place of Rumi's field.

I'll meet you there.

Charlie Morley

London, 31 October 2024

PART I

MEETING THE SHADOW

*'Loving oneself is no easy matter,
because it means loving all of
oneself, including the shadow.'*

JAMES HILLMAN[1]

There is a source of energy within us that contains the seed of awakening. We may hide it from others, though we know that it's there. Like fire, if ignored or misused, it may burn us, but if harnessed, it can warm us, protect us and revolutionize our life. We call it 'the shadow'.

In this first part of the book we're going to meet our shadow. By its very nature, the shadow is what we aren't conscious of, so to meet it we need to move into the realm of the *unconscious*. We'll use self-enquiry, guided imagination, dreamwork, drawing and creativity to do that, but first let's learn about what the shadow actually is and what shadow work can do for us.

CHAPTER 1

WHAT IS THE SHADOW?

'The truth of the matter is that the shadow is 90 per cent pure gold.'

CARL JUNG[1]

There are dozens of different definitions of the shadow. From psychologists to shamans, everyone has their own unique take on it. Buddhist meditation teacher Rob Nairn called it 'all the aspects of ourselves that we don't want to face'.[2]

Psychologist Stephen Diamond sees it as 'all that we deem unacceptable and deny in ourselves'.[3]

Shamanic practitioner Ya'Acov Darling Khan says it is 'anywhere that your fear becomes greater than your current capacity for love'.[4]

The concept of the shadow is found within almost every culture and spiritual tradition the world over, but it was first popularized in the West by the legendary Swiss psychiatrist Carl Jung. He used it to describe the part of the unconscious mind that was made up of all the seemingly undesirable aspects of the psyche that we had rejected, denied or disowned.

For Jung's protégé Marie-Louise von Franz, the shadow was 'simply the mythological name for all within me that I cannot (yet) directly know'.[5]

'The shadow' is a wide-ranging term, but in this book we'll use it to refer to anything within us that we are currently unwilling to extend our love to: the wounds, traumas and fears that are seemingly too painful to face and the inner gold, talents and power that are seemingly too brilliant to display.

The shadow *is* our dark side, but not 'dark' as in 'negative' or 'malign', rather 'dark' as in 'not yet illuminated'. It is comprised of everything within us that we don't want to face. That is, everything both seemingly harmful *and* potentially enlightening – all that we have rejected, denied, disowned or repressed.

So, the shadow isn't evil or bad, it's simply the parts of ourselves that seem incompatible with who we think we are.

Dark and Golden

Many people, when they first hear about the shadow, immediately think about their potentially harmful traits like anger, prejudice or hatred, or what might be considered unacceptable, such as sexual kinks or taboos. Interestingly, though, the shadow contains just as many – if not more – overtly beneficial traits, such as inner strength, beauty and talents, that have been kept hidden. So it has two sides: dark and golden.

The Dark Shadow

The dark shadow contains the traits that we deem to be negative or harmful and have rejected. It contains the answers to questions like 'What am I most afraid of?', 'What am I most ashamed of?' and 'What parts of myself do I struggle to love?'

The dark shadow is made up of all that we hide from ourselves and others, our seemingly unlovable parts: our fear, trauma, shame and prejudice.

The dark shadow is often misinterpreted as something bad or harmful, which leads us to invest energy in either denying it or trying to defeat it. The truth is, though, that the shadow is neither bad nor harmful, it is simply unintegrated energy, and until we learn how to tap into this energy, transform it and access its power, we will never become a fully integrated or fully authentic human being.

The poet Rainer Maria Rilke said, 'Perhaps everything terrible is, in its deepest essence, something helpless that wants our love,'[6] and so it is with the shadow. Becoming a shadow worker, as you will see, is all about love.

The Golden Shadow

The golden shadow (sometimes called the positive shadow) is made up of our hidden talents, our unseen beauty and our unfulfilled potential. It contains the intuition, creativity, childlike vitality and spiritual power that we rarely express.

Just as the dark shadow is made up of all the parts of ourselves that we fear may lead to rejection, the golden shadow is made up of all the bright, brilliant and magnificent parts of ourselves that we fear may be too great, too awesome or too challenging for others (or even ourselves) to see.

Just as it takes conscious effort to reclaim and transform the energy stored in our dark shadow, so we must make an effort to reclaim the golden shadow's energy if we are to be complete, balanced and authentically whole.

Jungian author Robert A. Johnson has said that to be willing to draw the skeletons out of the closet is quite easy, but to truly own the gold in the shadow can be much more difficult.[7] This is because the golden shadow challenges our limited self-image. Truly owning our highest potential and waking up to the brightness of our inner light is such a threat to who we think we are that our limited ego-mind will often do everything it can to prevent us from doing so.

Perhaps your golden shadow contains the esoteric side that you hide from others for fear of being labelled too 'woo-woo'. (I believe that's the technical term for it.) Or is it that blinding light of your spiritual potential that you daren't express for fear that it might isolate you from your friends or family? Maybe it's your innate intelligence that you play down for fear of seeming 'too clever'.

I know that for many people I've worked with their golden shadow contains the natural expression of their feminine sexuality, which they temper or hide for fear of being labelled 'too sexual' or 'too glamorous'. Interestingly, 'glamour' comes from the ancient Celtic word *gramarye*, which described the tangible enchantment of a woman's feminine power. So, as my *gramarye*-vibes-giving mum used to tell me: 'Never hide your glamour, darling!'

Where do you hide your light or limit yourself? What golden traits are you unwilling to love? What passions do you hide for fear of rejection? The answers to these questions will lead you to your golden shadow.

Many of us hold the unconscious belief that our golden shadow traits will lead to jealousy, suspicion or rejection if revealed. But, as Marianne Williamson famously said, 'There is nothing enlightened about shrinking so that other people won't feel insecure around you. We are all meant to shine, as children do.'[8] To own our golden shadow is to allow ourselves to shine.

Dark or Golden?

The dark and golden shadows are in fact different parts of the same thing. David Richo, in his brilliant book *Shadow Dance*, describes the dark shadow as 'a cellar of our unexamined shame' and the golden shadow as 'an attic of our unclaimed valuables'.[9]

It's not only our self-judgement that makes shadow content fall into one category or the other, but societal belief systems too. In some cultures 'vivacious individuality' would be classed as a dark shadow, whereas in others it would be classed as golden. Trans rights are blossoming across much of the world today, but many countries are introducing stricter rules around gender self-identification and sexuality than ever before. So we can see how in some cultures an issue can be viewed as a golden shadow that should be lovingly brought into the light, while in others it is seen as a dark shadow to be ashamed of.

The culture into which we are born insists that we behave in a particular manner, obliging us to disown all our 'unacceptable' traits if we are to be accepted by the tribe. It's interesting to note that the differences in shadow content between one culture and another can often contribute to conflict and strife on a worldwide scale.

The Collective Shadow

Although this book is primarily focused on integration of the personal shadow, it's important at least to address the concept of the collective shadow.

Carl Jung spoke not only of a personal unconscious, the aspects of our own mind of which we are unaware, but also of a collective unconscious, a vast storehouse of ancient human experience containing themes and images found cross-culturally throughout history. It is a kind of transpersonal library of the history and experience of all humankind, and it also has a shadow.

The collective shadow is made up of the dark side of society 'fed by neglected and repressed collective values'[10] such as racism, social taboos and fundamentalism. It also holds the repressed fear-based shadows of the world: war, environmental destruction, human and animal massacres, and our refusal to accept responsibility for integrating these.

The personal shadow is the bridge to the collective one, so becoming aware of our own shadow keeps us from 'falling into the mass psychosis of the collective shadow'.[11] When we integrate our own shadow, we not only contribute less to the projected chaos of blame, shame and pain that occurs in most human relationships, but we also add less to the collective shadow that fosters conflict on a wider scale.

So, the more people who integrate their shadow, the better for the world at large. By shining light into your own unilluminated shadows, you help light the way for others. As my Buddhist teacher Lama Yeshe Rinpoche says, 'To change ourselves is the only way to change the world.'[12]

In the next chapter we'll take a look at some more of the tangible benefits of shadow work, but for now let's recap what we've explored so far.

RECAPS AND REFLECTIONS

At the end of each chapter there will be recaps of key points and a few reflections too. You can write your answers to the reflections in the book itself if you like, or into a notebook or your phone. As you will be doing several writing exercises and keeping a dream diary as we progress through the book, it would be good to get yourself a separate notebook anyway, just for your shadow work.

Here are the recaps and reflections for Chapter 1:

✓ The concept of the shadow was popularized in the West by Swiss psychiatrist Carl Jung, born in 1875.

✓ The shadow isn't bad and we don't want to get rid of it, we want to transform it and harness its energy.

✓ Our dark shadow is like a cellar of our unexamined shame; our golden shadow is like an attic of our unclaimed valuables.

» How would you define the shadow if someone asked you right now?

» What is an aspect of your golden shadow that you hide from others and why?

» What do you think is one of the main shadows of the world right now?

» What is one shadow aspect that is seen as dark in one country and gold in another? Why do you think that is?

CHAPTER 2

WHY DO THE SHADOW WORK?

*'The cave you fear to enter holds
the treasure you seek.'*

JOSEPH CAMPBELL[1]

The shadow is a powerhouse of untapped energy, so becoming aware of its contents and transmuting its power are hugely beneficial to our psycho-spiritual growth. Although different traditions refer to it in different terms, any path that aspires to psychological wholeness will incorporate shadow work to some degree, simply because unless the shadow is integrated, the mind remains divided.

'To integrate' means 'to make whole, to bring together, to unite', and that's exactly what shadow work does. It consists of a series of practical exercises, meditations and shifts of perspective that help us to face and embrace the parts of ourselves that we have rejected, denied or disowned.

Medical News Today (yup, even mainstream medical websites now acknowledge shadow work) defines shadow work as 'a type of psychotherapy that focuses on the parts of the psyche that people often keep hidden, such as trauma and resentment'.[2]

The person who taught me about shadow work was Rob Nairn. He was a professor of criminology at the University of Cape Town and an expert on Carl Jung who packed in academia to become a renowned Buddhist meditation teacher, so he really knew both the dark side and the love and light side of the human condition.

He defined shadow integration as 'a process that enables unconscious psychological material to be recognized and accepted by the conscious mind, thus resulting in the beneficial release of that psychological energy into the wholeness of the psyche'.[3]

Sounds great, but what does that actually mean?

It means that through this work we become whole. It's crucial to remember that shadow work isn't about getting rid of the shadow, but integrating it. We want to harness its energy, not destroy it. And yet our aim isn't to act it out or indulge it either. This will simply solidify its separation from us. Instead, we want to befriend it and transform its power into healing energy and the energy of awakening. Although that may seem a bold claim, it is the sole aim of every exercise in this book.

Essentially, the result of shadow work is psychological wholeness, true authenticity and deep, lasting wellbeing.

And yet, most people just don't want to do it.

Fear of the Dark

Even the pioneer of shadow work, Carl Jung, knew that. His much-memeified quote 'One does not become enlightened by imagining figures of light, but by making the darkness conscious' actually has a second part to it that people rarely include. The quote continues with: 'The latter procedure, however, is disagreeable and therefore not popular.'[4]

That statement is perhaps even truer today than when he said it over 70 years ago. The often sanitized dilution of modern-day spirituality and the addiction to spiritual bypassing that plagues so much of the wellness scene confirms that many of us would rather drown in denial than truly see ourselves. But just as we can only see the stars at night, we must go into our darkness if we want to see our light.

At the shadow workshops and retreats that I run, even after hearing about how amazing shadow work is and how it can transform our lives for the better, some people still feel a bit scared about approaching their shadow and a few even worry whether it's safe to do so.

It's totally natural to feel a bit of fear around shadow work (fear is actually one of the building blocks of the shadow), but in fact integrating the shadow is the safest thing we can ever do.

The common approach to dealing with seemingly 'negative' emotions is to judge them, deny them and hide them from the world and from ourselves. This approach is unwise, though, because if we shove them into the recesses of our mind, they gather, gain power over us and erupt or spill forth when our guard is dropped. Sharing our headspace with an unseen and unloved shadow side is a recipe for agitation, anxiety and self-sabotage.

As Jung famously said, 'Everyone carries a shadow, and the less it is embodied in the individual's conscious life, the darker and denser it is,' and unless we integrate it, it may coalesce to 'form a mass, and from there emerges a raging monster'.[5]

It's true that the longer things stay in the shadows, the darker and denser they become, and yet once we're ready to shine light into the places that scare us, we can unravel decades of darkness in a single moment of clarity. This book will help you shine that light in a safe and contained way by gradually introducing you to your shadow. Follow the exercises step by step and take it as slowly as you need to.

Bear in mind that the shadow *wants* to be known and the mind *wants* to be integrated – that is a natural inbuilt predisposition – and they will only show you what you are ready for and no more.

So, if you're ready now, let's explore some of the benefits of this work.

Five Core Benefits of Shadow Work
More Authenticity

For me, one of the greatest benefits of shadow work is authenticity. I've been exploring the shadow for almost two decades now, and for over 10 years shadow work has been one of my main spiritual practices. So, do I now have a fully integrated shadow? Absolutely not. Have I faced and embraced all my demons? Not a chance. (I had no idea I had so many till I started this work!) So, what has shadow work done for me? It's made me a hell of a lot more authentic.

I got into Buddhism as a teenager and even spent seven years living in a Tibetan Buddhist centre with monks and nuns. Doing meditation retreats is a big part of the Buddhist path, as they allow you an intensive period of time to go deep into mind training without any distractions. At the end of 2015, I did a three-month retreat during which I was mostly alone, mostly in silence and mostly meditating and chanting all day. I soon discovered that when you do nothing but meditate all day, the shadow can be abundantly and quite shockingly revealed.

As the days turned to weeks, I came face to face with the essence of my dark shadow: the part of me that was a judgemental, neurotic control freak with addictive tendencies and an imposter syndrome. I witnessed what I came to refer to as my 'Magnificent Messiness' and my 'Fabulous Fuckedupness'. I became aware of the traumatized, angry, perverted and shameful parts of myself that I had denied and rejected for years in the hope of being a 'good Buddhist' – whatever that meant.

The more I looked, the more I saw, but strangely, the more I saw, the lighter I started to feel. I soon started to feel more confident, more real, more authentically myself.

And I saw the other side of myself too: my golden shadow, the part of me that was so brilliant and so bright that it was just as hard to look at and even harder to share.

By the end of three months, I knew beyond doubt that shadow work wasn't about fixing yourself or becoming 'good', it was about making friends with your mind, learning to love yourself and showing up authentically, as a beautifully imperfect human being in all your Magnificent Messiness.

More Energy

Ice baths, microdosing and bullet-proof coffee are good, but if you want access to an unlimited source of energy, look to your shadow.

The shadow is one of the most powerful energy sources in the human mind, and yet for many of us it is an energetic drain, because we waste so much energy trying either to deny it or destroy it.

Think how much energy we waste in trying to keep our shadow side hidden from others, or even denying that we have a shadow side. Imagine what life could be like if you could release and harness that energy?

The shadow is literally made of energy. Its contents, such as fear, shame and trauma, as well as unexpressed gold, joy and sexuality, are all huge sources of energy, and so anytime we integrate the shadow, we regain and release all that energy back into our consciousness.

This newly integrated energy may manifest as a kind of *bounce* or *uplift* within our creative centres as new ideas, sexuality, creativity and artistic inspiration start to emerge.

A guy on one of my shadow courses who worked as an energy healer told me, 'I feel as though I'm firing on all cylinders. I feel lighter, but more energized too. Something's definitely working here!' This was a textbook example of someone feeling the energizing effects of shadow integration.

More Compassion

Compassion isn't an activity we choose to do, it's a quality of being, a state of mind that aspires to see the Buddha beneath the bullshit in every person we meet, including ourselves.

Meeting and befriending our own unilluminated dark side isn't only the most compassionate thing we can offer ourselves, it's also the best method for working compassionately with the shadow sides of other people. Through opening up to our own pain and shame, we become more empathetic to that of others, as we realize that we may not all be in the same boat, but we are all in the same storm, and that everybody is trying their best.

It's been said that 'the shadow is the bridge to universal compassion'[6] and with compassion comes courage – the courage to shine light into the areas of our mind that we dare not look into and the compassion to accept what we find there.

We mustn't confuse compassionate acceptance with approval, however. To do so may limit the free expression of our compassion, as we wait to pass approval before offering it. We needn't approve of what or who we show love to, just be willing to offer our love regardless.

More Spiritual Growth

Shadow work produces a more mature personality and leads directly to spiritual growth. Full shadow integration, both dark and golden, isn't just a prerequisite for spiritual awakening, it's synonymous with it.

If we don't integrate our shadow, we may tend to have weaker or shallower psyches. That doesn't mean that we are weak or shallow people, simply that our psychological depth will be limited by the extent to which we have integrated our shadow.

Not everyone agrees with this, though. Some people feel that 'being spiritual' is about smiling all the time, posting 'good vibes only' on their socials and denying their dark shadow for fear of 'manifesting negativity'.

This tendency to overlook or minimize our unenlightened human condition in favour of a hitherto unattained spiritual ideal has a name: spiritual bypassing. It leads to stunted spiritual growth and a constricted, shame-based sense of who we are, which makes it impossible to progress on the path of self-development.

To really be all that we can be, we have to do something that may seem revolutionary to the 'good vibes only' crowd: we have to own our shit and do the shadow work. That's *real* spiritualty.

More Changing the World

This final benefit may seem a bit extra, but shadow work really can change the world.

You are an interdependently linked being, so every change you make, every insight you have, will immediately resonate out to all the people around you. When you do any form of psycho-spiritual work, this immediately dovetails into the hearts of those close to you. So, every change we make, every shadow we integrate, will undoubtedly impact upon the wider world.

And beyond that, imagine if our world leaders were practising shadow integration? Imagine if when Kim Jong Un met Donald Trump he was aware of his father/authority figure shadow being triggered. Or he could see that Trump reflected some of his golden shadow around wanting to be a person of the people. It's just a silly example, but it does strike me that so much of the conflict in the world, both at a local and a geopolitical level, is based upon our leaders' fundamental ignorance of their own shadow material.

RECAPS AND REFLECTIONS

✓ Integrating your shadow side is the safest and greatest gift that you can offer the world.

✓ The most compassionate – and radically authentic – thing you can do is be yourself. In all your Magnificent Messiness.

✓ Shadow work is the direct opposite of spiritual bypassing – it asks you to own your shit and take full responsibility for who you are while working towards becoming all that you could be.

》 What benefits do *you* hope to gain through shadow work?

》 Do *you* have any fear of working with your shadow side?

》 How do you think shadow work could change you for the better?

In the next chapter you're going to encounter your first shadow work exercise, so before you do, I invite you to set your intention for this work.

If you're reading this book, it's probably safe to say that what you intend to do is to learn and practise shadow work, but *why* do you want to do it? What made you pick up this book in the first place?

Are you sick of patterns from your past stifling your future happiness? Have you finally had enough of being judgemental and unkind to yourself? Do you want to further your spiritual growth or to be more authentic? Or to reclaim your shadow energy, or to fulfil your highest potential?

Whatever your reasons, take a moment to set your intention by by filling in the blank below:

I want to work with my shadow side because _____

_____

_____

CHAPTER 3

SEEING THE SHADOW

'[This] thing of darkness I acknowledge as mine.'

WILLIAM SHAKESPEARE, *THE TEMPEST*, ACT V, SCENE 1, LINES **267–76**

We are about to explore a set of questions that will bring us into a direct meeting with our shadow side.

This can be prickly work. It's like exploring a rose bush – you will find great beauty, but occasionally you may encounter a thorn. So, please go slowly, be gentle with yourself and maintain a sense of playfulness.

As you do the exercises in this book, especially some of the ones in Parts II and III, you will at times feel challenged as you see the side of yourself that you usually hide, so be sure to talk through your experiences whenever you need to with a trusted friend, therapist or coach.

The questions may well challenge you, as they are questions that many of us spend our whole lives trying to avoid answering. And then, if we do answer them, we so often deny the answers.

But whatever your answers are, remember that your shadow is simply the part of you that is yet to be loved, so compassion, rather than judgement, is all that you need to integrate it.

Exercise: Dark Shadow Questions

This first set of questions will help you meet some of the aspects of your dark shadow.

Step 1

Take a moment to come into an awareness of your breath. Just notice when you are breathing in and notice when you are breathing out.

Notice three breaths before you begin.

Why not just jump straight in? Think of the mind as a lake, the questions as pebbles and the answers as ripples that the pebbles make when you drop them into the lake. If you want to see the ripples clearly, you need to make sure the surface of the lake is calm before you drop the pebble.

Step 2

Answer the following 10 questions without too much deliberation – the first answer that comes is often the truest, but feel free to have several answers to each question. Note down your answers, either digitally or in your notebook. You won't be asked to share the answers with anyone, so please answer freely without self-censorship. Give yourself no more than a couple of minutes for each question (too much time and you might start self-censoring).

1. What am I most afraid of?

2. What am I most ashamed of?

3. What lies about myself do I tell others?

4. What parts of myself do I hide from others?

5. What parts of myself do I struggle to love?

6. What personal habits, obsessions or addictions cause me pain?

7. What secret do I hope nobody ever finds out about?

8. What part of my body am I least happy with?

9. What groups of people do I have prejudice towards?

10. What are the themes of my anxiety dreams or nightmares?

Step 3

Make a list of the key points from your answers, entitled 'Aspects of My Dark Shadow'.

You may end up with a list that looks something like mine:

Aspects of My Dark Shadow

– Failure/exposure/letting people down/unfair blame

– My past habits/the way I used to be

– That I'm stronger than I am/better than I am/gentler than I am

– My old habits/violent rage/my loneliness/knowledge/ sexual kinks and porn

– Loneliness/guilt complex/sexual trauma

- Judgemental thinking/guilt complex/porn/sexual objectification

- REDACTED (it's a secret!)

- My skinny legs

- Right-wingers/posh jock-type men/New Agey people

- Heartbreak trauma/Losing control at workshops (used to be my mum dying)

Step 4

Remind yourself that nothing on your list is 'bad' and you don't want to get rid of it. It is simply unintegrated shadow content that you can now see clearly.

Read through your list and take a moment to consider how each answer makes you feel. Your body may notice something that your mind has missed, so as you read through the list, do you notice any somatic response – a change in your breathing or a tightening of your body or a desire to move or fidget?

If so, just notice, for example, *Oh wow, I felt a real freeze response when I read the word 'failure'* or *My mouth really dried up when I saw the answer that said 'loneliness'.*

Remember, your shadow isn't bad, it's simply the parts of yourself that you are unwilling to love, and that everything on your list, however seemingly harmful, will have a helpful element within it.

Step 5

And finally, as a way of letting your shadow know that you see it, read through the list of answers and say to each of them, out loud if you can:

'I see you, my shadow.'

The three words 'I ... see ... you' hold huge amounts of power.

Remember, the shadow *wants* to be known, so once you've let a shadow trait know that you see it, its power over you diminishes.

Exercise: Golden Shadow Questions

Now here are some questions to help you meet some aspects of your golden shadow.

Be sure to keep your answers to both these sets of questions, because you will be referencing them in later exercises.

Step 1

Take a moment to come into an awareness of your breath. Just notice when you are breathing in and notice when you are breathing out.

Notice three breaths before you begin.

Step 2

Answer the following 10 questions without too much deliberation – the first answer that comes is often the truest, but feel free to have several answers to each question.

These questions are a bit more abstract than the dark shadow questions, so feel free to interpret them in whatever way you like.

Note down your answers, either digitally or in your notebook.

Again, give yourself no more than a couple of minutes for each question.

1. What things in life bring out the best in me?

2. What golden parts of myself do I hide from others?

3. If I didn't need to work for money and could spend my life 'following my bliss' (my true passion), how would I spend my life?

4. In what social situations do I play small or tone myself down?

5. Based on a playful amplification of my own personality, if I had one superpower, what would it be?

6. What aspects of myself was I forced to hide or shut down in childhood?

7. What things in life make me feel alive?

8. Who do I most admire and why?

9. In what areas of life do I hide my light or limit myself?

10. What do I want to be when I grow up?

Step 3

Make a list of the key points from your answers to the questions above, entitled 'Aspects of My Golden Shadow'.

You may end up with a list that looks something like mine:

Aspects of My Golden Shadow

- Being kind/teaching/helping people

- Love of singing/chaplaincy

- Teaching/learning/mind expansion/helping people/
  surfing

- Dinner parties with 'real adults' (used to be in front of
  my step-siblings)

- Infinite enthusiasm!

- My loudness/my enthusiasm/my long hair

- Being kind/loved ones/bringing joy/dancing/play

- Lama Yeshe for his journey/veterans for their sacrifice

- Spiritual practice

- Enlightened (or a rock star)

Step 4

Read through your list and take a moment to consider how each answer makes you feel. Your body may notice something that your mind has missed, so as you read through the list, do you notice any somatic response – a change in your breathing or a tightening of your body or a desire to move or fidget?

If so, just notice, for example, *Oh wow, I felt such a deep sense of relief in my body when I read through the things that I was forced to hide in childhood* or *I felt choked up when I read my superpower.*

Step 5

Remind yourself that your golden shadow is simply the parts of yourself that you are yet to activate fully.

And finally, as a way of letting your golden shadow know that you see it, read through the list of answers and say to each of them, out loud if you can, 'I see you,' and to any qualities that you want to activate and start to embody, 'I see you. I activate your potential.'

Dedication

If it feels right to do so, take a moment to dedicate the beneficial energy of this exercise to yourself and to all beings, using the statement:

> 'I dedicate the beneficial energy generated by this exercise to the benefit of all beings.'

The Seeing Is the Doing

Now that you're aware of some of the aspects of your personal shadow, you might well be thinking, *What do I do now? What can I do to fix this stuff?* Or *How do I step into my gold? What can I do to manifest my potential?*

For now, in this early stage of your work, you need do nothing more than recognize and bear witness to your shadow side with compassion for integration to start to occur. Recognition is the key.

This forms the basis of what the Indian philosopher Krishnamurti famously referred to as 'the seeing is the doing' – the idea that awareness is, in and of itself, transformative.

Let's unpack this a bit more. So much of our harmful behaviour can be traced back to unseen and unrecognized shadow material: 'I don't see my anger, so I project it onto others and see them as threatening' or 'I don't recognize my divine potential, so I have low self-esteem.' This shadow material can be integrated through any practice that allows us to *see* the shadow aspects that were previously *unseen*.

By seeing, witnessing and recognizing our shadow content, we not only gain freedom from the potentially harmful effects of projecting that unseen energy onto others, but we also harness that energy to fuel the fire of our spiritual growth.

In fact, in the Buddhist teachings it is said that the basis of our unawakened state is a habitual unwillingness to *see*, because the act of seeing, the act of recognizing and the act of waking up require emerging from the duvet of denial that we are forever trying to sleep under.

RECAPS AND REFLECTIONS

✓ At this stage you're simply meeting the shadow, so there's nothing to change and nothing to fix.

✓ Remember, 'the seeing is the doing'. Awareness in and of itself is transformative.

✓ *'I see you'* are words of power that let your shadow know that you are ready to meet it.

» How was it to explore those shadow questions and did you find the golden or the dark shadow questions easier to answer?

» How many of those questions did you know the answer to already?

» How would you feel if someone read through your answers?

» Is there something that you can do today to help you step into the gold that lies within your shadow side?

CHAPTER 4

SEEING THE SHADOW IN OTHERS

*'We do not see things as they are.
We see things as we are.'*

RABBI SHEMUEL BEN NACHMANI[1]

Projection is something that we hear a lot about in the wellbeing scene, but what is it?

It's a psychological defence mechanism whereby we unconsciously place or 'project' our own unacceptable psychological qualities onto others.

It is also the main method of communication that the shadow uses to make itself known to us. And so, one of the most direct ways of meeting our shadow is by seeing how we project it onto others.

Projection Reveals the Dark Shadow

Rob Nairn once told me, 'We unconsciously push away what we don't want to feel and what we think will harm us. These may be very small things – annoyances, upsets, emotional wounds, embarrassments and rejections – but just as small drops fill a big bucket, soon we have a heavy reservoir of rejected psychological energy weighing us down, and to try and lighten the load we start to project it out onto others.'[2]

Dark shadow projection is a huge subject, so we are going to focus primarily on the three main types.

'It's Not Me, It's You'

It's annoying to even admit it, but what irritates us most in other people is often indicative of what we are unwilling to recognize and accept in ourselves. Essentially, people who really piss us off are often those who display a quality that we are pissed off or ashamed that we have within ourselves.

The psychotherapist David Richo nails it when he says: 'What strongly repels us in others is a clue to where our own darkness lurks.'[3] He explains that the disliked features of our own personality are indicated by repulsion and aversion towards those who demonstrate those very traits.

From this perspective, being triggered into annoyance can actually be very enlightening for us and lead to deep insights into ourselves.

Okay, but how can we tell the difference between shadow projection and somebody just being an idiot?

Sometimes being annoyed is a genuine response to someone doing something that is genuinely annoying or unjust. However, when our level of annoyance far outweighs the annoying action, then almost certainly a shadow projection has been triggered within us. An inflated or disproportionate emotional response is almost always indicative of projection.

Some people worry that awareness of projection will turn them into human doormats refusing to act against injustice because 'It's all just my projection.' In fact, the opposite is true. Once we know the true nature of our shadow projections, we can respond to situations more effectively because we know that our actions are not driven by projection and so we can trust our judgement more.

As Keila Shaheen says in her book *The Shadow Work Journal*, 'When you're triggered, it can feel as if you're reacting automatically, without a conscious choice,'[4] so becoming aware of our triggers gives us more choice and more autonomy.

Transpersonal psychology pioneer Ken Wilbur has a model for recognizing shadow projection. He says, 'If a person or thing in the environment *informs* us, we probably aren't projecting. On the other hand, if it *affects* us, then we probably are.'[5]

Let's say I see someone drop litter. If my peace of mind remains pretty unaffected, even though I may discern that their action is unwise and even decide to act upon what I have observed by disposing of the litter myself or challenging them on their actions, there is probably no shadow projection. If, however, I experience an inflated emotional response disproportionate to the act, such as yelling, whether internally or externally, 'People like that shouldn't be allowed to walk the streets!', then I can be sure that there is shadow projection around the act of dropping litter.

'It can't be shadow projection, I've never littered in my life!' you may protest. In that case, try and focus less on the act itself and more on the *energy* of the act. This is vital when looking at shadow projection: focus on the *energy*, not the *act*.

In the case of littering, the energy might be one of selfishness and lack of regard and respect. You may never have littered in your life, but can you really say that you've never acted selfishly or with a lack of respect?

Reminded of Who We Used to Be

Another type of shadow projection, and one of the most triggering for many people, is when we react to unacceptable traits that we used to display but believe that we don't display any more.

For example, we are more likely to have a disproportionate emotional response to the arrogance of another person if we used to act arrogantly ourselves. Why? Because they are reminding us of a shameful part of ourselves and being reminded of our past shame triggers us into offence.

An over-exaggerated emotional response also shows that the change in our behaviour isn't fully integrated, because if it was, we wouldn't be so easily triggered by those who continue to act that way.

In fact, as holistic psychologist Dr Nicole LePera says, 'Sometimes, we may even virtue signal when we're around those people to cope with the internal conflict of not accepting those aspects of ourselves.'[6]

This form of projection can work with more virtuous traits too. The 'happy-go-lucky' positivity of another person might irritate us if we used to be like this ourselves, but are no longer that way as a result of depression or distressing life experiences, for example.

In fact, this type of projection often feeds in to the next type we're going to explore.

Secretly Wishing to Be That Way

Finally, there is the projection of seeing a trait in another person that we secretly, and often unconsciously, want to display ourselves, but daren't. This one has caught me waist-deep in shadow projection more times than I care to remember.

Let me explain. One of my main annoyances in life used to be self-appointed gurus who said whatever they liked and then proclaimed its 'ultimate truth' because it was 'channelled from a higher power' (one that only they had contact with) and thus 'beyond dispute'. This kind of behaviour used to really trigger me. After exploring other explanations, I had to consider the uncomfortable possibility that perhaps there was part of me that wished that I could do the same.

Was there really a part of me that secretly wished I could just teach or write what I liked rather than go through the often rigorous academic study and spiritual training that are required in Tibetan Buddhism? Although it makes me cringe to admit it, it was definitely true. In fact I could see multiple times when I'd done similar things to those 'gurus' but been too ashamed to admit it.

Once I was aware of this particular shadow projection, though, I could at least crack a little smile when I felt myself being triggered, and slowly, over time, I could begin to let it go. I still get triggered by this sometimes, but at least now I am triggered from a place of greater awareness and humour than before. It's been a long road, though.

Ken Wilbur believes that 'the shadow is not an affair between you and others but between you and you'[7] and that until we recognize and befriend our projected shadow, we will erroneously see it in everybody else but not ourselves.

Once we are conscious of our shadow projections, we can be kinder, more loving human beings, because we not only see how we are projecting onto others, but also how they are projecting, and with that we don't have to take everything so personally any more.

We can even learn to become fascinated when we catch ourselves projecting, even amused. A feeling of *Oh wow, this guy is really triggering my shadow!* can provide humour that acts as a buffer zone, allowing us to respond consciously rather than react unconsciously.

The key takeaway is that the next time something or someone really annoys you, before reacting, take a moment to ask yourself these three questions:

1. 'Am I ever like that?'

2. 'Have I ever been like that in the past?'

3. 'Do I secretly wish I *could* be like that sometimes?'

Very often the answer will be in the affirmative to all three, and with that you will gain insight into your shadow side and might even feel a bit less annoyed too.

Projection Reveals the Golden Shadow

Just as our dark shadow is projected onto others, so is our golden shadow. Crucially, though, it appears not as irritation, but as *admiration*. We are still triggered by someone but rather than being triggered into annoyance, we are triggered into adulation and awe.

The traits we admire in others are often our own disowned or unrecognized potential. Any strong or overexaggerated feeling of admiration or idolization for someone is often indicative of the projection of our own inner gold.

So, anytime you find yourself gushing with praise for someone or really idolizing another person, take a moment to ask yourself, 'Am I ever like that?' and 'Do I have the potential to be like that?'

Just as we may fear the dark shadow, so we may be in awe of the golden, as the talents, potential and unseen capacity within us are projected onto those whose capacities we admire. But, as psychology professor Geoffrey Lantz told me, 'If you recognize and resonate with the greatness in someone else, then you inherently have that greatness within yourself, otherwise you wouldn't be able to recognize it in the first place!'[8]

Science backs up this theory too. A study published in the *Journal of Personality and Social Psychology* found that a person's tendency to describe others in positive terms was an important indicator of the positivity of their own personality traits.[9]

Golden shadow projection displays itself in many different ways, but the three main forms are:

- *Golden traits that we deny we have but aspire to:* 'I can't dance very well, but I've always wished I could.'

- *Golden traits that are already activated, but yet to manifest fully:* 'Yes, I totally get what you're saying. Dancing is all about freedom. I really resonate with that. I can't dance well, though. No, I'm not a dancer.'

- *Golden traits that we used to have and wish we still had:* 'You remind me of myself at your age – I used to love dancing. I had great energy, just like you.'

So, anytime you feel your heart open in admiration, resonance or joyful congratulation, you can be sure that the energy of what you are admiring, resonating with or congratulating will also be found within you and is waiting to be expressed.

Exercise: The Projected Shadow

How can we reclaim those parts of ourselves that we have been so busy projecting onto other people? How can we accept and express the talents and brilliance that we hide?

The first step is to recognize those traits. This exercise (inspired by David Richo's *Shadow Dance*) will help you do exactly that.

Step 1

Take a moment to come into an awareness of your breath. Just notice when you are breathing in and notice when you are breathing out.

Notice three breaths before you begin.

Without thinking about it too much, and definitely without censoring yourself, list three traits, either digitally or in your notebook, that you strongly dislike and that really trigger you about members of the following groups:

- the same sex as you
- the same profession or those who have a similar life path to you
- the same nationality as you
- the same generation (millennial, Gen Z, etc.) as you
- the same race as you

Step 2

Now, list three traits you really love and admire about members of the following groups:

- the same sex as you

- the same profession or those who have a similar life path to you

- the same nationality as you

- the same generation (millennial, Gen Z, etc.)

- the same race as you

Step 3

Read through both the dislike and admire lists and take a moment to ask yourself:

- 'Do I ever embody any of these traits and if so which ones?'

- 'Have I ever embodied any of these traits in the past and if so which ones?'

- 'Do I ever wish that I *could* embody any of these traits and if so which ones?'

- 'Do any of these traits appear in my dreams and if so which ones?'

Step 4

If you like, you can add some of the things that you answered 'yes' to in Step 3 to your 'Aspects of My Dark Shadow' and 'Aspects of My Golden Shadow' lists as they will probably be part of your own shadow.

Dedication

If it feels right to do so, take a moment to dedicate the beneficial energy of this exercise to yourself and to all living beings, using the statement:

> *'I dedicate the beneficial energy generated by this exercise to the benefit of all beings.'*

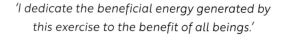

As with the previous exercise, you might be feeling a burning desire to change or fix these projections that you are now aware of, but at this stage on your journey you just need to be more aware of your shadow projections than you were before. That awareness is all that's needed now.

Zen Buddhist master Thích Nhất Hạnh used to say, 'Awareness is like the sun. When it shines on things, they are naturally transformed.'[10] So there's no need to do anything now but be aware of those projections.

Creating Reality

I want to finish this chapter with a personal story.

I first started teaching lucid dreaming and shadow work when I was 25, and I felt anxious and unsure of myself. I thought that people would judge me and not take me seriously because I was so young. The years of training I had done with well-respected teachers were completely drowned out by my own anxiety. Once, while teaching at a Buddhist centre in Wales, I created an entire *external* reality based on an illusory projection of my *internal* anxiety.

Let me explain. As I started to teach the more complex Buddhist aspects of lucid dreaming, I began to feel anxious and worried that I might not get it right. Just as the anxiety set in I noticed a woman in the back row making strange facial expressions, grimacing even, each time I concluded a relevant point.

This grimacing went on throughout my talk. It was as if every time I made a salient point or even a little joke, she would scowl, while everyone else would smile or nod in agreement. There were 20 people in the audience and 19 of them were enthusiastically engaged, but my mind was 100 per cent focused on the one person who seemed to be confirming how I felt inside.

Soon my head was spinning. *I knew I shouldn't have tried to teach the complex stuff! This woman hates me! She obviously knows more about it than I do! I'm a fraud!*

At the tea break I decided to do the shadow work by walking straight over to talk to her.

To my surprise, before I could even introduce myself, she had broken into a warm lopsided smile and said how much she had enjoyed the first session.

As a teenager, I used to volunteer at a charity that read books to people who had had strokes, so I had spent a lot of time with stroke survivors, and up close it was clear that this woman had had a stroke and that when she smiled, it looked (at least from a distance) a little bit like a grimace. She wasn't grimacing, she was smiling!

And *that* is how projection works.

My apprehension about teaching the complex Buddhist stuff had been projected onto the audience, where it had latched onto a misconception of reality that supported its perceived truth. Through projection, I had created an external reality that supported my internal one and, with that, I understood the words of the Buddha himself: 'With our minds we make the world.'

RECAPS AND REFLECTIONS

✓ When looking at shadow projection, focus on the *energy*, not the *act*.

✓ If you recognize and resonate with the greatness in someone else, then you must have that greatness within yourself.

✓ Even a smile can be seen as a scowl when you are projecting!

》 Anytime you are triggered by another person (either into irritation or admiration), ask yourself:

- 'Do I ever embody these traits?'

- 'Have I ever embodied these traits in the past?'

- 'Do I sometimes wish that I *could* embody these traits?'

》 What celebrity do you really crush on or admire and why?

》 How might being aware of projections help you in your relationships?

》 When was the last time you caught yourself projecting?

CHAPTER 5

THE CHILDHOOD SHADOW

*'We can easily forgive a child who is afraid
of the dark; the real tragedy of life is
when adults are afraid of the light.'*

PLATO[1]

C arl Jung believed that we weren't born with a shadow, we created one, and this process began in childhood.

Looking at our childhood is delicate work, so please be gentle with yourself.

I acknowledge that many people have experienced some form of childhood abuse, be it mental, emotional or physical. However, it is not within the scope of this book (or my expertise) to safely explore and incorporate the painful shadow effects of childhood abuse. Instead, this book focuses upon working through the more general shadows that are most commonly experienced in childhood. Whatever comes up for you though, please seek the help of a qualified therapist or trusted friend if you feel you need support.

Let's explore three of the main ways that we create our shadow in our early years.

The Checklist of Love

For the first few years of life, a human baby is totally dependent upon its primary caregivers. This is a unique trait. It means that a human infant is uniquely programmed to adapt its behaviour to please its primary caregivers (usually its parents), because it has to if it is to survive. Essentially, the child starts to create a checklist of what brings love from its caregivers and what brings lack of love. This binary forms the basis of the ego (our sense of self) and the shadow.

The child notices that if it does what its caregivers want it to do, it receives affection and love, and so it does more of it. Being angry and throwing toys however, might lead to the removal of love, so the child learns that its anger is bad and starts to believe that anger must go into the shadow and 'being nice' must go into the sense of self.

Some of the first shadow content that Western children create is often around nakedness, as we realize that being naked in public is frowned upon. So we disown our nakedness and force it into the shadowy 'cellar of the unacceptable'.

Body shame may soon be joined by anger and greed, both of which we're taught are unbefitting for 'good' little boys and girls to display.

This whole process is inherently culturally specific – the child of progressive parents who value free expression will have a very different checklist from a child of strict, conservative parents – but naturally, the child soon starts to equate being good with being loved. This is an equation that leads directly to unhappiness. Our innate goodness as a human being has nothing to do with the opinions of the two people who happen to be our parents.

Burying Our Treasure

In many ways, creating a checklist of love plays an important role in our development, because without love we might be abandoned and unable to survive.

However, the problem is that we struggle to separate the different aspects of our emotional energies. So, if we are forced to bury our rage – because rage is not on the checklist of love – we may inadvertently bury some of our assertiveness too, and if our sexuality gets buried, part of our creativity may go with it.

The same process occurs with our golden shadow. Being a great dancer or having lots of charisma may have been seen as a threat to our social compatibility when we were children, so we may have been forced to bury these golden treasures in our shadow side.

As a child, I was often being told by teachers and sometimes my parents, 'No need to shout, Charlie!' or 'Calm down, don't be so loud!' and so I received the message (loud and clear) that expressing my enthusiasm and joy for life was bad and would lead to the removal of love, and so I should bury that golden trait away.

From a psychological perspective, the formation of our sense of self is created in response to the culture around us, which requires us to trim off the top shoots of our highest potential and bury the gold that is too heavy to carry if we are to sit neatly within the hedgerows of social normality.

No Stranger, No Danger

In a child's mind, the 'stranger danger' concept is not seen to be applicable to its parents or primary caregivers. This plays an important evolutionary role, as it allows us to bond with our parents in a much deeper way than with other members of the tribe. But it also means that the personal opinions of our parents are in most cases not taken as mere *opinions*, but are installed in our unconscious mind as *facts*. So when our parents offer a critical or unhelpful opinion about us – 'You can't dance' or 'You're not clever' – we don't question it, but instal it directly into our psychological operating system.

As the brilliant holistic psychologist Dr Nicole LePera says, 'When we are children, we don't have discernment about what to take personally and what not to take personally. Everything is taken literally and directly. If someone we love very much (whom our survival depends on) tells us that we are doing something "bad" or "wrong," we may come to believe we are bad or wrong.'[2]

When I first encountered this idea, I was shocked. It suggests that every time a young child hears an opinion from a parent, caregiver or authority figure, they may well accept it as truth and allow it to shape their emerging sense of self.

Inevitably, our parents add to our shadow even more when they project their own unintegrated shadow onto us. In her book *Daring Greatly*, Brené Brown mentions a client who loved art as a child but once overheard his uncle say to his father, 'You're raising a faggot artist now?' as he pointed at his artwork taped to the refrigerator. The little boy never painted again, but his inner artist will still be there, waiting for him in the light of his golden shadow.[3]

Musing on this point, shadow expert Robert A. Johnson believes that integrating our own shadow is the greatest gift we can give our children, because in so doing we are offering them a clean psychological heritage.[4]

The Bag That We Drag Behind Us

The American poet Robert Bly was a pioneer of shadow work. He was also a brilliant writer on the subject and came up with one of the best descriptions of the shadow that I've come across. He called it 'the bag that we drag behind us'.[5]

Riffing on the concept of 'psychological baggage', he saw the shadow as a huge sack full of our fear, shame, secrets, talents, inner power and gold that we drag behind us through life.

Bly believed that we came into this world 'baggage free' but created 'the bag that we drag' as children as a way of keeping our parents' love by shoving our seemingly unloved parts into the bag, safely out of sight of Mummy and Daddy.

By the time we go to school our bag is already quite large, and then, as authority is transferred to our teachers and to children of a higher status, their opinions dictate what we stuff in there.

By adulthood, we have become so accustomed to stuffing anything we don't want to show to others into our bag that we continue doing it simply out of habit. I suggest that we break this habit and reclaim the gold that lies in our bag.

As children, we place all the parts of ourselves that are deemed 'not good' into the bag. But we shove in much more besides. Anything that isn't on the checklist of love goes into the bag. All of the gold that we are forced to bury goes into the bag. Some children are forced to put the loud *enthousiasmós* of childhood in the bag, and with it goes their *joie de vivre*. Others are told to put their anger in the bag, and with it goes their assertiveness and decisive clarity. Some grow up being taught that sex is shameful and so they put their sexual energy in the bag, along with much of their vitality and creativity.

Every time we consign something to our bag, we lose energy. The psychological energy, the *chi*, that lies in anger, joy, sexuality and desire is lost when we stuff them into our bag.

The job of the shadow worker is to open their bag and look closely at what it contains. By doing this, we will understand that a lot of it isn't needed any more and we can start to unpack our bag, unload our psychological baggage and regain the energy that we lost in childhood.

Exercise: What's in Your Bag?

Our first two shadow work exercises were based around 'self-enquiry': using questions that we don't usually ask ourselves to access parts of our mind that we don't usually access. This exercise, though, is much more of an art therapy one. It asks you to use drawing as well as words to help uncover your shadow.

Again you won't be asked to share your bag with anyone, so be as open and uncensored as you can.

Step 1

Find yourself a sheet of paper and at least one pen (the more, the better!)

Take a moment to come into an awareness of your breath. Just notice when you are breathing in and notice when you are breathing out. Notice three breaths before you begin.

Step 2

Draw a picture of yourself as a child in one of the bottom corners of the page. A simple stick-person drawing is fine, but be more elaborate if you like.

Next, draw a bag or sack somehow attached to your image of yourself as a child.

Take a moment to review what you have drawn so far. How did you draw yourself as a child? Smiling and happy or with no face at all? Is it an accurate representation or yourself or is it fantastical? What does the image you have drawn tell you about yourself as a child?

Now look at your bag. Is it optimistically small or does it take up the whole page? What does the size of the bag you have drawn tell you?

Step 3

Now, using images and words, add in the contents of your bag. What parts of yourself did you consign to your bag during childhood? Your loudness? Your joy? Your love of singing? The wounds from the bullies at school? The disapproval of your parents? Write them in the bag.

What parts of yourself weren't on the checklist of love? Write them in the bag.

Step 4

Now add in all that you have put in your bag in your adult life: heartbreaks, career failures, break-ups, grief and all the other aspects of emotional baggage that are currently weighing you down.

Add the parts of yourself that you don't yet love and that you hide from others – the shame, traumas, fears, unlived dreams, taboos and secrets. You might like to use your answers to the 'dark shadow questions' (see p.22) for reference.

Write in the bag *anything* that is weighing you down.

Step 5

And now, add the gold that you have lost to the bag – the parts of yourself that are too bright, too audacious, too authentically 'you' to share with others. Add in the parts of your golden shadow that weigh you down. Gold is heavy, and hiding our golden shadow can be just as heavy a burden as hiding our dark shadow.

You might like to use your answers to the 'golden shadow questions' (*see p.25*) for inspiration.

Don't censor yourself – be honest and courageous. You don't have to share the contents of your bag with anyone. And, as with all these exercises, you can't get this wrong. If there's something that weighs you down, whether seemingly helpful or harmful, add it to your bag.

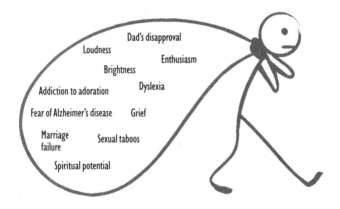

The bag that we drag

Step 6

Once you have added everything you can think of, take a moment to look through the contents of your bag and remind yourself that nothing there is 'bad', it is just either unintegrated or yet to be activated.

Ask yourself the following questions:

- 'How much of the bag's contents was I aware of already?'
- 'What do I feel when I look into my bag – shame, regret, authenticity, joy?'
- 'How would I feel if I were to reveal the contents of my bag to others?'

Step 7

Now find a way to send loving awareness to the contents of your bag. You might like to recite an affirmation of loving acceptance such as:

'I see you.'

As always, 'the seeing is the doing', so simply by becoming conscious of the contents of your bag, you will start to lighten its load.

Dedication

If it feels right to do so, take a moment to dedicate the beneficial energy of this exercise to yourself and to all living beings, using the statement:

*'I dedicate the beneficial energy generated by
this exercise to the benefit of all beings.'*

••

Seeing ourselves clearly may initially be uncomfortable, as we see things we'd prefer not to see – arrogance, fear, shame, unlived dreams – but, as the Buddhist teacher Pema Chödrön reminds us, 'These are not sins, but temporary, workable habits of mind, and the more we get to know them, the more they lose their power.'[6]

Exercise: Helium Balloons

This next exercise builds upon the previous one and asks you to add some balloons to your bag.

Step 1

Using your 'Bag That We Drag' drawing, draw several helium balloons above your bag with their strings attached to it. If you don't have enough space to add these in, stick another piece of paper onto the top of your current one (*see below*).

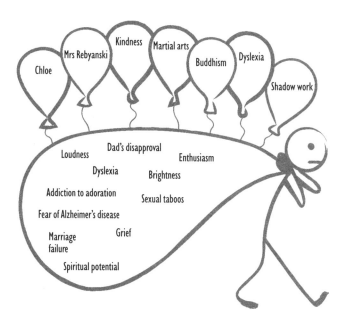

Lightening the load that we drag

Step 2

In a few of the helium balloons, write or draw anything that helped you to carry that heavy bag through your childhood – things that lifted you up, lightened your load. These could include people, pets, objects, activities, hobbies, family members or teachers from your past or present. Anything or anyone that helped that bag feel lighter and your childhood more bearable.

Step 3

Now, draw in another few balloons, and in each one, write or draw whatever helps you as an adult to lighten the load of your psychological baggage.

Again, this could include people, pets, objects, activities and hobbies, as well as spiritual practices, aspects of your sexuality, psychedelics, ice baths, sweat lodges, psychotherapy or whatever helps you to lighten the load of your bag.

Some of your balloons might actually be quite destructive too. One guy I worked with wrote 'food addiction' in one of his balloons because he very honestly admitted that this addiction lightened the load of the depression that was weighing down his bag.

You can also add in some of the things from your 'Aspects of My Golden Shadow' list, perhaps including your superpower and what you want to be when you grow up.

You may find you have something that appears in both your bag and your balloons. Those of us working with neurodiversity may find that our particular place on the spectrum might be both a heavy burden and a load-lightening balloon.

Step 4

Take a moment to look at your helium balloons and explore the following questions:

- 'How many of the balloons was I aware of already?'

- 'What do I feel when I look at the balloons – gratitude, melancholy, joy, surprise?'

- 'How able am I to reveal the contents of my balloons to others?'

Step 5

Now, find a way to send loving acceptance and gratitude to your helium balloons. You might like to recite an affirmation of loving acceptance such as:

> *'I see you. I show you my love.'*

Step 6

Take a moment to witness both your bag and your helium balloons.

Dedication

If it feels right to do so, dedicate the beneficial energy of this exercise to yourself and to all living beings, using the statement:

> *'I dedicate the beneficial energy generated by this exercise to the benefit of all beings.'*

. . . .

Real-Life Feedback

After doing these exercises at one of my workshops, a woman called Nikki, who works as a change management consultant, emailed me, saying:

> 'As they say, "Shit gets real" when you turn inwards and I've felt that something has shifted. I feel more present now and less shackled by my demons.
>
> I've struggled with addictive and impulsive behaviour since my teens, but through this work I've been feeling more positive about integrating this stuff.
>
> Actually, this is the first time I've really had a proper look at my shadow self and recognized it's not as scary as I'd thought.'

Other workshop participants told me how grateful they felt when they realized how many balloons they had in their life, while another woman told me how sad she felt that she couldn't think of one human being to have as a balloon. Hers were all pets or animals.

As with so many of these exercises, it's not so much the exercise itself that leads to the insight, but the act of reflecting on the exercise. So, with that in mind, here are some more reflections, along with some key points about our childhood shadow.

RECAPS AND REFLECTIONS

✓ We start to create our shadow in childhood.

✓ As children we often instil the opinions of our parents as if they were facts.

✓ Every time we consign something to our bag, we lose energy.

✓ The job of the shadow worker is to open their bag and look closely at what it contains.

» What golden treasure were you forced to bury in childhood?

» Can you think of a specific parental opinion about yourself that you have instilled as a fact?

» If you have any specific people in your balloons, do they know that this is the role they play (or have played) for you?

» Were all of your helium balloons overtly positive or did you have any that were actually harmful but nonetheless helped to lighten your load?

CHAPTER 6

MEETING THE SHADOW IN DREAMS

'All human beings are also dream beings.
Dreaming ties all mankind together.'

JACK KEROUAC[1]

I f you want to know your shadow, you need to know your
dreams.

I've written three books on lucid dreaming and sleep practices,
so as you might expect, dreamwork is a key component of my
approach to shadow integration.

When we dream, the shadow, both dark and golden, can be
displayed openly and without the censorship of the waking mind.
So, if we open up to our dreams, we open up to our shadow.

Our shadow actually wants to be known and so it will display
itself in our dreams in the hope that we will recognize it,
because through that simple act of recognition it will begin to
be integrated.

Dreaming of themes related to our shadow is a very good sign, but when the dark shadow displays itself at maximum volume, we may label the experience a nightmare and in our aversion miss the opportunity to recognize and integrate it. (In Chapter 10 we'll start to reframe this aversion.)

Carl Jung said, 'The human mind is divided into two parts, the conscious and the unconscious, with the unconscious being by far the larger of the two.'[2] The unconscious contains huge stores of information, to which the conscious mind has very limited access in the waking state. But the unconscious is revealed in our dreams, so by recalling them we gain access to that information.

Our unconscious mind often uses the themes, characters and symbols of our dreams to highlight areas of ourselves of which we are unaware and which require integration. Shadow material forms a large part of this.

So how does this actually work? While we're awake, the sentinel of the ego-mind (which is constantly blocking unacceptable shadow material from arising) is almost always on guard, but for those two and a half hours of dreaming each night, the sentinel sleeps at its post and the shadow material from the unconscious can be displayed openly and without censorship.

When we dream, we are a captive audience for the shadow's play. The theatre doors have been locked by our circadian rhythms and we have no choice but to witness the shadow's performance.

And it's not just dark shadow material that will be displayed. When our golden shadow reveals itself we might dream of joyful situations, hanging out with our favourite celebrities or people we idolize, and wake up feeling full of energy and inspiration after what we might label 'an amazing dream' full of positive symbolism.

But what, you may say, if you don't dream? Don't worry – everybody dreams. Based on an average eight-hour sleep cycle, most people have four or five dream periods every night, but not everybody remembers their dreams. Why? Often simply because they don't try to remember them. Most people find that with a little effort they can soon start to recall their dreams. Here's an exercise to help direct that effort.

Exercise: Boosting Dream Recall

If we set a strong intention to recall our dreams before we go to sleep each night, most of us are able to recall at least part of them without too much difficulty. It often shocks people how easily they start remembering their dreams once they actually try to.

These five steps will have you recalling your dreams in no time:

Step 1

Set your intention to recall your dreams before you start dreaming. Before bed and then as you're falling asleep, recite over and over in your mind:

'Tonight, I remember my dreams. I
have excellent dream recall.'

Step 2

Try waking yourself briefly during a dream period, so that the dream is fresh in your mind. When do dream periods occur? Dreaming is part of every 90-minute cycle of sleep, but the last two hours of your sleep cycle are when your longest dream periods occur.

Step 3

Often, dream memories are felt in the body as well as held in the mind, so don't forget to explore any bodily feelings that you wake up with. Sometimes dream recall can be as simple as:

> *'Can't remember much of the dream, but I woke with a feeling of happiness in my belly.'*

Step 4

If you can recall just one image from a dream, you can work backwards from that point and eventually gather the rest of it. As soon as you wake up, ask yourself:

> *'Where was I? What was I just doing? How do I feel?'*

Step 5

Don't give up if you can't remember a dream straight away. Give yourself the time and space to remember. The memory might not appear until hours after you've woken up.

The most important of these five steps is the first one: set your intention to remember your dreams by mentally reciting, as you fall asleep:

> *'Tonight, I remember my dreams. I*
> *have excellent dream recall.'*

If you do this every night for a week, you'll soon break even the strongest dream blackout.

If you haven't remembered a dream for years, just recalling a tiny fragment of one is a great success, so work from where you are and don't put too much pressure on yourself to remember every dream straight away.

....

Many people find that shadow work has a noticeable effect on their dreams and so it's a good idea to keep track of your dreams as you go.

Writing Down Your Dreams...

By writing down your dreams, you'll start to see your shadow displayed on the page before you. So, keeping a dream diary is a must.

Exercise: Five Steps to Keeping a Dream Diary

Keeping a dream diary is simple. Here's how to do it:

1. Whenever you wake up from a dream, recall as much of it as you can and then write it down or document it in some way. Many people like to type their dream recollections into a smartphone, while others like to use a notebook and pen. Either method is fine, but if you are going to

use a digital device, make sure the screen brightness is turned down low to avoid too much sleep-disturbing blue-spectrum light.

2. You don't need to record every detail – you'll know what feels worth noting and what doesn't. Focus on the main themes and feelings, the general narrative and any strange anomalies or notable shadow content that you can recall.

3. If you wake up in the middle of the night after a vivid dream, try to make a few notes there and then, because you might have forgotten the dream by the morning.

4. Try and write something in your dream diary every morning if you can, even if it's just: 'I know that I've been dreaming, but I can't remember what about.'

5. You don't need to spend ages documenting your dreams; in fact, you'll be surprised how much you can write up in just five minutes. I rarely spend more than that writing down my dreams at night, but I often expand them further over breakfast.

If you're new to dreamwork, don't be disappointed if you only remember a few snippets of each dream. That's fine for now. Work from where you are and gradually you'll start recalling more and more.

In Part II you'll learn how to decode your shadow material from your dreams, but for now you just need to get the firm basis of dream recall and keeping a dream diary.

••

Meeting the Shadow

And finally, to end our 'Meeting the Shadow' section of the book, let's add a guided imagination exercise to our toolbox of techniques.

We're going to imagine actually meeting our shadow in personified form.

We'll do this by imagining that our shadow sides, both dark and golden, come and sit with us. Then we're going to visualize welcoming them, taking them by the hand and sitting with them in friendship.

Don't worry about whether you can visualize clearly, just relax into the immersive feeling of imagination.

Exercise: Meeting the Shadow

I recommend doing this exercise using the 'Meeting Our Shadow' guided meditation that you can find on my website (www.charliemorley.com/shadowexercises), but if you would like to follow it without guidance, this is the full script:

Step 1

Just sitting, with your eyes open or closed (either is fine), breathing through your nose or mouth (either is fine), breathe deeply. Show your body that you love it enough to give it what it needs: breath.

You are totally safe. You are held lovingly by the beneficial motivation of this meditation. Relax deeply – deeply enough to look into your shadow.

Step 2

Take a moment to think about the unloved parts of yourself that you find unacceptable to show to others.

Think about the parts of your mind that you struggle to love: your anger, your fear, your past traumas, aspects of your sexuality that you fear may be frowned upon perhaps.

Take a moment to consider and to encounter the dark shadow parts of yourself.

If shame, guilt or discomfort come up, don't turn away from them as you have done before, turn towards them.

Step 3

Find the place in your body where the dark shadow is located.

Imagine that your dark shadow flows out of your body and manifests in physical form on your left-hand side.

What does it look like? Does it have form or is it formless? Does it have a gender? Is it a human, an animal or perhaps something else?

However it manifests, your dark shadow is sitting next to you on your left-hand side. It will only show you what you are ready for, so feel its energy fearlessly and greet it like an old friend.

Step 4

Take your shadow by the hand and sit with it. Friendship starts with a smile, so smile at your shame, your fear, your guilt, or whatever form the energy takes. Encounter this energy with love. Hold its hand. Nothing more is needed. Feel it responding to your love.

Step 5

And now take a moment to think about all the magnificent parts of yourself that you find unacceptable to show to others. Is there a part of yourself that you find too bright to show to others? Your true potential, your intuition, your divine light?

Take a moment to encounter these golden shadow parts of yourself.

If power, joy or strong energy come up, don't turn away from them as you have done before, turn towards them, greet them like old friends. They are part of you.

Step 6

Find the place in your body where the golden shadow is located.

Imagine that your golden shadow flows out of your body and manifests in physical form on your right-hand side.

What does it look like? Does it have form or is it formless? Does it have a gender? Is it a human, an animal or possibly something else?

However it manifests, your golden shadow is sitting next to you on your right-hand side. It will only show you what you are ready for, so feel its energy fearlessly and greet it like an old friend.

Take your shadow by the hand and sit with it. Friendship starts with a smile, so smile at your divine light, your power, your golden potential... Encounter this energy with love. Hold its hand. Nothing more is needed. Feel it responding to your love.

Step 7

And now, sitting between the dark and golden shadows, repeat after me, in your own mind, three times, the following words:

'I am ready to love my shadow. I am ready to befriend both the dark and the bright.'

Step 8

Allow the visualization to dissolve so that you are now sitting alone again.

Dedication

With the knowledge that you have just connected lovingly with both aspects of your shadow, take a moment, if it feels right to do so, to dedicate the beneficial energy of the meditation to yourself and all beings, using the statement:

'I dedicate the beneficial energy generated by this exercise to the benefit of all beings.'

• •

RECAPS AND REFLECTIONS

✓ The shadow *wants* to be known and will appear in your dreams in the hope that you will recognize it.

✓ By recalling our dreams, we start to see the shadow on its own turf: the unconscious mind.

✓ By writing down our dreams, we pay homage to them and, more importantly, reinforce the habit of viewing them as something valuable.

» What appeared when you imagined your dark and golden shadows?

» How did it feel to imagine meeting your shadow in personified form?

» How does it feel to have completed the first part of our journey together?

» Are you ready to go deeper now that we have laid down the basics?

PART II

BEFRIENDING THE SHADOW

'There are no strangers here; only friends you haven't yet met.'

W.B. YEATS[1]

Shadow work asks us to look at things that we usually shy away from or reject, but, as the Tibetan Buddhist teachings say, 'If you reject an emotion, it will become your enemy. If you indulge it, it becomes the boss of you. So what do we do with our emotions? What's the best method? Face them and make friends with them!'[2]

Cultivating an attitude of friendliness towards ourselves and others lies at the core of shadow integration. Unconditional friendliness towards our vulnerabilities and our strengths, towards our darkness and our light, and, crucially, towards those who, however painfully, expose our shadows is vital to the process.

Whether dark or golden, our shadow is simply the unintegrated parts of ourselves, so to make friends with our shadow is to make friends with ourselves.

And what is the driving force of this friendliness? Kindness. Be kind. Actively seek out ways to show kindness to yourself and your shadow. Friendliness, kindness and compassionate acceptance lie at the core of this work.

As we move into Part II we are going to need to harness all three of these as we learn about the building blocks of the shadow, explore the masks that we wear and transform our perspective on nightmares. The warm-up is over, so buckle up and let's move into befriending our shadow.

CHAPTER 7

ACCEPTANCE, FORGIVENESS AND GRATITUDE

'Forgiveness is the fragrance that a violet sheds on the heel that crushes it.'

ANON

Who we are is not our fault, but it is our responsibility. Fortunately, our *ability to respond* to our current shadow is not predicated on the actions of the past, but on our willingness to accept and forgive in the present.

As we look at the contents of our bag and at how much of it was stuffed in there during childhood, and we remember the things that were said to us, the wounds that were inflicted on us and the limiting critical programs that were installed in our mind, we may inevitably come across anger, blame and bitterness. This is totally natural, and anger can be a very clarifying emotion, but blame and bitterness only lead to more shadow.

We might well say, 'Why did they behave that way? It was completely unacceptable!' and yet our ability to move forward depends largely on the extent to which we *can* accept the seemingly unacceptable things that have happened to us. Not condone, but accept.

Acceptance

Shadow work is fundamentally about showing love to that which we are yet to love. Acceptance and love are closely linked, because to accept yourself fully is to extend your love to every part of yourself, however shadowy some of them may seem.

Psychologist Robert Holden, PhD, says, 'It's the emotions that we judge the most, that we are the most ashamed of and most afraid of, that we must meet with the most acceptance. With acceptance, something starts to change in the shadow. It starts to transform.'[1]

Paradoxically, once we can accept that we have certain shadow traits within us and are brave enough to tell them, 'Okay, I see you and I accept that you are part of me,' they actually start to diminish.

Crucially, the use of the word 'acceptance' here does *not* mean the approval or endorsement of harmful mind-states or damaging situations. Imagine we have broken our toe. We don't have to *approve* of having broken our toe, but we do have to accept that it is broken before we can start healing it. If we don't accept that it's broken we won't be able to apply the correct methods to heal it.

So, acceptance of what has happened to us – not *approval of*, but *acceptance of* – is a prerequisite to healing – and to shadow integration.

Forgiveness

Forgiveness is also a vital part of healing, but what is it exactly and how does it relate to the shadow?

Robert Holden specializes in this field, and explained, 'Whatever you haven't forgiven is your shadow. The shadow is made up of whatever you are unwilling to show love to, and what you don't forgive, you don't love. The process of forgiveness is to bring love to what you haven't forgiven. It arises from the willingness to bring love to a situation.'[2]

Brooding over past grievances can be like picking a scab: if we do this, it will never heal.

Lack of forgiveness makes us afraid, cautious, less likely to embrace life fully. We fear that we may be wounded again and will have another wound to carry, so we don't risk it, we play safe.

Holding on to resentment towards a person is like letting that person have control over our nervous system. Constantly going over what we want to say to someone we haven't forgiven is allowing them to live rent-free in our head. And worse of all in both these cases, that person doesn't even know that we're hating on them, so they are happily getting on with their life while we're still chained to the past.

When I shared this with Robert, he said, 'Exactly! Forgiveness sets us free. We don't forgive to be spiritual or good, we do it to be free. To forgive is to decide that "From this moment forward I will not be limited by that grievance. I will still feel it, but I will not be limited by it." There has to be a moment when we think, *Is holding on to this grievance helping me any more or just weighing me down?*'[3]

And yet many of us actually don't want to forgive. Why is this?

'Who Am I without My Wounds?'

Our ego identity is sometimes threatened when we forgive. It may ask, *Who am I without my grievances? Who am I without my resentment?* These questions challenge who we think we are and so make us feel uncomfortable.

Robert believes, 'We have resistance to forgiveness and even fear of it – a fear founded on the misperception that if we forgive, we are *condoning* the unforgivable action and letting the other person get away with it.'[4]

If we feel this resistance, then it is important to meet the part of us that doesn't want to forgive and to ask ourselves quite a radical question: 'If I were to forgive this person, or even myself, which part of me would be disappointed?'

Often the person we are most unwilling to forgive is ourselves. We might feel that self-forgiveness is undeserved and that we are somehow helping the person we have wronged by maintaining our guilt and shame. In fact, the opposite is true, for it is our guilt that energetically connects us to the wronged person, and so when we release our guilt and forgive ourselves, we release that person too.

I've often struggled with forgiveness. I'd convince myself that I'd forgiven someone, but whenever their name was mentioned, a kind of mental pop-up would appear, reminding me of the past grievance, complete with the date when it occurred and a brief synopsis of the unforgivable deed. And with that I would cringingly have to admit to myself that I hadn't fully forgiven them. Part of me had, but not the whole of me.

But even if only 1 per cent of us is willing to forgive, that can be enough to begin with. The love that forgiveness brings will begin to seep in slowly, drop by drop, and eventually bring us back to a place of love.

Gratitude

On the flip side of forgiveness, we find gratitude. Reviewing the content of our bag might ask us not only to forgive people from our past, but also to thank those who helped us. These people were not only vital guides and catalysts of our potential, but also often golden shadow reflections of ourselves.

Did you write someone's name in one of your helium balloons? Has looking at your baggage triggered a memory of someone who helped you to unpack it?

These allies often see a reflection of their own inner light in ours and so they know what we are truly capable of before we do. And yet how many of them have we taken the time to thank, truly and fully, for what they have done for us? How many of these catalysts of our true potential have we acknowledged as such?

In the next exercise I want you to think back to the people who helped you in the past, maybe in childhood or more recently, and explore your gratitude towards them.

To take time to do so is to pay homage to the golden allies in your life and to use gratitude to access the gold that lies within you.

Exercise: The Gratitude Letter and Visit

In this exercise I invite you to acknowledge and pay homage to the people who helped you by writing them a gratitude letter and then, if possible, thanking them face to face and reading the letter to them.

This practice has some great mainstream evidence to back it up. Research conducted in the field of positive psychology has shown the 'gratitude visit exercise' makes people happier and less depressed for weeks and even months afterwards.[5]

Through this letter and visit, you not only offer thanks to those who helped you, but also integrate your golden shadow and ask it to offer you its energy even more fully than before.

Step 1

Take a moment to come into an awareness of your breath. Just notice when you are breathing in and notice when you are breathing out.

Notice three breaths before you begin.

Step 2

Select one important person from your past who helped you or perhaps saw your golden potential even before you did. Maybe it was someone who believed in you when nobody else did? Maybe it was a teacher from school or a friend who was there for you when nobody else was?

Take some time to relive the memory of exactly what this person did for you and consider how their support helped to manifest your golden shadow potential. Maybe without their support you would never have started following your passion? Or maybe it was their help that gave you the confidence to step into your gold?

Step 3

Write a short letter to that person, which you are willing to share with them, describing how they helped you and thanking them for their help. Be specific and write down exactly what it was that they did to help you.

You don't have to mention shadow work if you feel it may complicate things. The power of this exercise comes from paying homage to the beneficial potential that they helped you to unlock and then by showing gratitude to *their* inner light for doing so.

Step 4

As soon as possible, find a way to communicate the contents of your letter to that person. If you can, go and visit them and share it face to face. That would be best. If that's not possible, then you can do it over the phone or send them the letter or email it. Even if you haven't spoken to them for decades, reach out, find them, make the effort and you will reap the rewards.

Once you have shared the contents of the letter, allow the person to respond unhurriedly and give yourselves time to reminisce about the events in question and how they impacted upon both of your lives.

If they feel too shy to respond or if they block the process, that's fine. The process doesn't actually require their participation to work.

If the person has died or is uncontactable, you can read your letter out loud to a photo of them, or even just remember them and imagine what their response might be.

....

The first time I did this practice was with my meditation teacher Rob Nairn. It was clear to me that my entire career could be traced back to the opportunity he had given me when I was 25 years old and he first asked me to give a talk at one of his workshops.

After he read the gratitude letter (he was teaching at the time, so I couldn't share it face to face), he came over to me with watery eyes and said, 'That was the kindest thing anybody has ever written me.'

We then sat and reminisced about what I had written in the letter.

Since then I've written gratitude letters and made gratitude visits to estranged friends, old teachers, mentors, family members and those who had helped me in ways I had yet to fully thank them for. None of those relationships have ever been the same again. Once you open up with vulnerability and truly show people your gratitude, your hearts are entwined forever.

Attitude of Gratitude

Gratitude is good for you. Scientific research has shown that the easiest way to maintain our levels of happiness, regardless of socio-economic standing, is to live with an attitude of thanks and gratitude towards life. Harvard researchers found that just two minutes of intentional gratitude practice for 21 days in a row could actually rewire the brain to work more optimistically and more successfully.[6]

Taking stock of – and writing down – what you're grateful for every day can help you focus on what you have in your life, instead of focusing on what you don't have, or what you 'think' you need for a happy life.

Gratitude is not only scientifically proven to be beneficial, but also a great way to unlock the energy within our golden shadow, so I suggest we start to practise it now with this fun but powerful exercise.

Exercise: 21 Days of Gratitude

This exercise asks you to document the things that you are grateful for each day as a way of cultivating a new perspective on life that is infused with gratitude.

Step 1

At the end of each day write on a Post-it note three things that you've been grateful for that day. These could be anything, great or small, but make them personal to you and try to have three new things each day. Anything from 'I had a really good coffee this morning' to 'I had a huge spiritual breakthrough' can be included.

Step 2

Stick the Post-it note up on a wall or mirror.

Step 3

Do this for 21 days in a row, so that you have 21 Post-it notes grouped together by the end.

Step 4

After 21 days, read through all your Post-it notes and allow yourself to really tune in to the gratitude of the past three weeks.

Then, if you like, take a photo of your collection of Post-it notes and share it on your socials with a short description of the exercise so that others can try it as well. You can tag me in the photo too, if you like.

RECAPS AND REFLECTIONS

✓ Shadow work is fundamentally about showing love to that within us which we are yet to love.

✓ Acceptance doesn't mean approval or endorsement of negative mind states or situations. It is, however, a prerequisite to actively engaging with negative situations and doing something about them.

✓ When we forgive, we aren't letting the other person 'get away with it', rather we're letting ourselves be free of them.

✓ Harvard researchers have found that just two minutes of intentional gratitude practice for 21 days straight can actually reinforce neural pathways associated with positive emotions.

》 Who are you ready to forgive?

》 How did it feel to write the gratitude letter?

》 Are you ready to start the 21-day gratitude challenge? If so, note down three things you are grateful for today right now.

》 Have you been keeping up your dream diary? In Chapter 10 we will be learning how to decode our shadow from our dreams.

CHAPTER 8

UNDERSTANDING THE BUILDING BLOCKS OF THE SHADOW

*'Whenever we suppress a feeling or deny
a part of ourselves, we create shadow, and
as we go through life, we are doing this
constantly... pushing away what we don't want
to feel and what we think will harm us.'*

ROB NAIRN[1]

Every time we shame ourselves or others, every time we turn away from what scares us and every time we push away the parts of ourselves that have been wounded by trauma, we create shadow material.

And so the building blocks of the shadow are primarily made up of shame, fear and trauma. To truly befriend our shadow, we need to get know what it's made of, so let's look at each one of these now.

Shame

Shame, in its purest expression, is the feeling that what we have done is going to make us unworthy of love.

Although often used interchangeably with guilt, shame is actually quite different. Guilt says, 'I've done something bad,' but shame says, 'I am bad.' Guilt, although not always the most helpful emotion, at least has an active component in that it allows us to apologize and change our future behaviour constructively, whereas shame is inactive and stagnant and its secrecy negates the opportunity for constructive change.

Shame makes up a large percentage of our shadow material, both dark and golden, whether it's sexual shame relegated to the dark shadow or the shame of not fully expressing our truth that we have forced into the golden one.

In her book *Daring Greatly*,[2] shame researcher Brené Brown, PhD, offers three main perspectives on shame, which can be summarized as:

1. Everybody has it – it's a universal emotion.

2. We are all afraid to talk about it.

3. The less we talk about it, the more power it has over us.

She believes that it all boils down to this: shame gains its power from being unspeakable.

And so awareness of shame and the courage to speak it out loud can in large part rob it of the power it has over us. Shame is like a vampire: not only does it survive by drinking our life-force, but it fears the light and burns up under the glow of conscious awareness. This is why so many shadow work practices (including the one in the next chapter) involve recognizing and talking about our shame.

Shame is closely linked to fear – the fear that others will discover our shame and the fear that what we are ashamed of will make us unlovable.

Fear

Anything within us that we are afraid of or that we are afraid to look at forms part of our shadow. Shadow work is fundamentally about making friends with what scares us: our darkness, but also our light.

Fear can be defined as 'the anxiety caused by our anticipation of a perceived threat, real or imagined'. It is an inbuilt response to physical or emotional danger, and if we didn't feel it, we couldn't avoid or protect ourselves from threats to our survival, so fear isn't bad. It becomes a hindrance only when we fear experiences and situations that aren't current threats to our survival. For example, the reason that fear of public speaking is so deeply entrenched in our minds is because when we were living as hunter-gatherers, being rejected by the tribe was a death sentence, and so we would fear anything that might subject us to such rejection. Today that is no longer applicable, but the fear lingers on.

Fear is one of the greatest obstacles to living a fully engaged life, and fear of our own shadow is one that most of us carry.

Fear is what keeps us from the mountaintop. It is not lack of fear that gets us there, but courage. Courage is not the absence of fear but the willingness to make friends with it. So often fear is a mile wide but only an inch deep. From a distance it seems to be a huge ocean that will drown us, but once we step into it, we realize that it is much shallower that we thought.

Moving courageously into the places that frighten us forms the basis of both dark and golden shadow work.

THE SCIENCE OF PHOBIAS

Professor of psychology Robert Leahy believes that almost all of the most commonly recognized phobias have links to our evolutionary history. He says, 'Agoraphobia [fear of open spaces] is related to our ancestors' vulnerability to predators in exposed open settings and some elements of post-traumatic stress disorder almost certainly originated as a way of keeping us away from dangers we'd already experienced as witnesses or near-victims.'[3]

Dr Fredric Neuman, director of the Anxiety and Phobia Treatment Center in New York, says, 'Phobias are best treated by exposing the affected person to the phobic situation a little at a time and for a long enough time for the fear of that situation to go away.'[4]

This well-known technique of gradual exposure to the phobic situation, known as 'exposure therapy', is one of the most effective and long-lasting treatments. This process of moving towards the fear as a way of habituating ourselves to it is classic shadow work and can be applied to the parts of our own mind that we are scared of too.

Trauma

Since the first iteration of this book back in 2017, trauma and awareness of the trauma that so many of us carry have exploded into the mainstream.

So, what is trauma? Trauma is the result of any stressful experience that overwhelms a person's ability to cope and to integrate their response to that stressful experience.

Many of the effects of trauma – anxiety, depression, hyper-vigilance, sleeplessness – are caused not so much by the trauma itself, but more by the dysregulation of the nervous system that the trauma creates.

Crucially, it is an individual's *subjective experience* that determines whether an event is traumatic or not. Some people are traumatized by a warzone experience, others by social media bullying. A broken heart can be worse than a death for some, and a pet dying can be worse than losing a human family member for others. Trauma is highly personal.

But trauma is trauma, whether from a military warzone or the familial warzone of a childhood home. If an event has such a strong impact on you that you are overwhelmed by the stressful effects and unable to integrate them, then that absolutely counts as trauma, so please don't feel that your trauma isn't 'enough'.

Much of the time, just as with physical wounds, our innate healing capacity naturally integrates our psychological trauma, so often trauma symptoms fade away within a few days or weeks of the traumatic event. And, just as a naturally healed physical wound sometimes leaves a scar, so do our psychological wounds, and those scars can often become a roadmap guiding us to our shadow.

PTSD

Sometimes, a certain trauma hits us much harder, lasts much longer and affects us more acutely than any other we have suffered. We might have flashbacks in which we relive or re-experience aspects of the trauma, or high levels of anxiety and hypervigilance, recurring nightmares, significant behavioural changes, crippling depression or numbing dissociation that not only overwhelm our ability to cope but, crucially, don't seem to fade with time. This is when our experience might start to meet the criteria of PTSD: Post-Traumatic Stress Disorder.

For almost 10 years now, I have worked with military veterans and other highly traumatized groups of people, and I have found that the 'D' for 'disorder' in PTSD is often unhelpful. As we go through a traumatic incident, almost all of us will experience a high level of distress and fear. This has an 'aftershock' effect on our nervous system, which might result in nightmares, anxiety, depression or feeling scared to visit the place where the incident occurred or to do the activity that led to the trauma. This is a hardwired part of our physiology, totally natural, and in no way a disorder.

For some people, though, a diagnosis of PTSD can be a blessing, as it provides a helpful label to explain what they have been going through, while for others it becomes a heavy burden of perceived shame or brokenness.

This book isn't designed for any form of self-diagnosis, so be sure to seek help and guidance from medical professionals if you feel that more information about PTSD would be helpful to you.

However, whether you have experienced trauma so debilitating that it meets the criteria of PTSD or not, if a distressing event has overwhelmed your capacity to cope, then that trauma will almost certainly form part of your shadow.

So how do we start to befriend these energies of shame, fear and trauma that so often hide in our shadow side? Through a process of kindness, friendliness and compassionate acceptance that the exercise in the next chapter will facilitate.

RECAPS AND REFLECTIONS

✓ Shame gains its power from being unspeakable.

✓ Courage is not the absence of fear, but the willingness to make friends with it.

✓ Trauma is trauma, whether from a military warzone or the familial warzone of a childhood home.

» How do you feel in your body when you experience shame?

» Can you think of a time when telling someone about a secret shame made you feel better?

» Which fear takes up the most space in your shadow?

CHAPTER 9

DROPPING THE MASKS THAT WE WEAR

'Tear off the mask. Your face is glorious.'

RUMI[1]

I uploaded the photo and instantly felt the fear. I knew that was the whole point of the exercise, but it didn't stop me feeling it.

I'd just uploaded a photo of a mask. On the outside of the mask I'd written the personality traits I presented to the world, but on the inside I'd exposed my deepest and most shameful shadow traits. I'd just revealed both sides of that mask to literally tens of thousands of people over three social media channels.

Would it be too much for the 'love and light brigade' to handle? Had I just thrown my career away? Would I be asked to leave the Buddhist centre where I was living? I was supposed to be a teacher, a role-model even, but now people knew the side that I hid from others: a scared boy with imposter syndrome who watched porn and sometimes liked to fight.

Seriously regretting what I had just done, I thought it best to remove the post. I reached for my iPhone to delete the photo, but then *ping, ping, ping*, 'likes' were suddenly coming in one after the other, and then comments: 'So real and raw', 'Beautifully authentic' and 'Awesome honesty, thanks for sharing!'

People actually liked it. In fact they loved it. Within the hour I was being tagged in the posts of people who had been so inspired that they had made their own masks and were uploading them to their social media feeds in solidarity.

By the end of the day, that photo was my most liked, most shared and most commented on social media post ever. It turned out that on seeing me share my shadow side, people felt empowered to start accepting theirs and move out of shame into the deep authenticity that lay behind the masks.

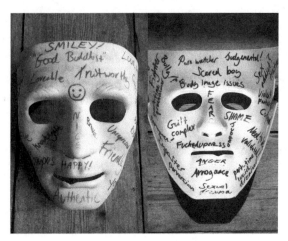

The masks that we wear

What I saw in my mask didn't shock me. I knew most of what I'd been hiding, just as you know most of what you're hiding, but what did shock me was how strong the aversion was when I considered sharing it with others. Still, I knew that strong aversion indicated strong suppressed energy, and that if I could release and transmute that energy, I could find gold within.

That incident was almost 10 years ago now and since then I've done this mask exercise dozens more times and shared my shadow publicly with thousands more people. Each time I do it, I feel freer, less ashamed and more tolerant of both myself and others.

Fascinatingly, I've found that sharing the shameful habits written on the inside of my mask has actually helped to release me from many of those habits. For example, the 'porn-watcher' bit is the shameful trait that often gets the most response at my workshops and leads to discussion about shame, masturbation and the internet generation. Interestingly, once I was able to admit publicly to this embarrassing present habit and former addiction, it actually had the effect of drastically reducing its occurrence. Why? Because shame *perpetuates the disconnection* that the addiction is trying to relieve.

When we shame ourselves or are made to feel ashamed about our addictions, we feel disconnected and are thus more likely to continue seeking out the connection we gain from indulging the addiction. But when we move into the vulnerability of witnessing our seemingly shameful habits and showing them love, our addiction to them wanes.

THE SCIENCE OF SHAME

Science has proved that shame perpetuates addiction because addiction is often based on a misplaced and unfulfilled need for bonding and connection that the thing that we are addicted to provides.

An experiment first conducted at Simon Fraser University in Canada way back in the 1970s showed that when you offered water with morphine in it to isolated rats in empty cages, they all drank it and almost all overdosed and died from it. But when you offered it to rats in a cage that was full of other rats and nice food and things to do ('Rat Park', as the researchers called it), they almost never drank it and none of them got addicted to it.[2] Why? Because they had connection and bonding. When we feel connected, we don't tend to get addicted to things or to create nearly as many destructive habits.

This theory was applied to humans in Portugal, with exactly the same effect: injecting drug use declined by 50 per cent because the money spent on shaming drug-users was spent on helping them bond and reconnect with society.[3]

Although the Rat Park experiment has been seen as an oversimplification by some, as someone who spent four years working as a drugs and alcohol outreach worker and who has struggled with addictive tendencies towards sex and recreational drugs myself, I have seen first-hand how shame really does perpetuate addiction and how transforming shame can help to treat it.

The *Persona*

The exercise we're about to do asks us to look at both our shadow and our *persona*.

The *persona* is a psychological term for the side of ourselves that we show to others. It's basically a portion of the ego, the portion that we are willing to reveal to others.

Carl Jung defined the *persona* as 'a kind of mask, designed on the one hand to make a definite impression upon others, and on the other to conceal the true nature of the individual'.[4] So the mask of our *persona* is indicative not only of the self-image that we present to others, but also of what we hide from them. And as long as we keep hiding behind the mask of who we think we *should* be, we'll never be free.

Most of us put all our energy into avoiding admitting that we have any seemingly shameful shadow traits and instead try and convince everybody that we are the happy, smiling *persona* that we show on our social media feed. We daren't enter into the vulnerability of the human condition. This leads to a constricted, shame-based sense of self.

Once we start to integrate the shadow and drop the mask, however, we have more energy, more authenticity and more empathy as we realize that we are all hiding behind a mask. So, I invite you now to drop that mask and see your original face as we prepare to explore the Two-Faced Mask.

Exercise: The Two-Faced Mask

When considering shadow integration, the pioneer of archetypal psychology, James Hillman, thought of it as a problem of love and asked: 'How far can our love extend to the broken and ruined parts of ourselves, the disgusting and perverse?'[5]

This practice is a powerful way to unmask the shame you hide, befriend your shadow, extend that love and step into your fully authentic self.

Step 1

Buy a white paper or plastic mask like the one in the photo on p.96 or, if that's not possible, make yourself a mask out of a piece of paper or card.

Get some marker pens with which to write on the mask too.

Step 2

Take a moment to come into an awareness of your breath. Just notice when you are breathing in and notice when you are breathing out.

Notice three breaths before you begin.

On the outside of the mask, write or depict all of the qualities that make up your *persona* – how you like to present yourself to the world. These may be true qualities, but they may also be more aspirational ones, or even just plain untrue. But don't censor yourself – just go for it. You can't get this stuff wrong.

When we do this exercise at my workshops, I usually give participants about 10 minutes for this step.

Step 3

Now, on the inside of the mask, write or depict all of the seemingly shameful traits, habits, secrets, taboos and dark shadow aspects that you hide from others.

If you like, you can write some of the contents of the bag that you drag behind you into your mask.

Feel free to add in some of the answers to your dark shadow questions such as 'What am I most ashamed of?' or 'What am I most afraid of?'

Really try and write every single thing that you hide from others in the mask, because the more you write, the more you see, and the more you see, the more you release!

Step 4

Now, still on the inside of the mask, write or depict aspects of your golden shadow that you hide from others.

The inside of your mask might end up containing just as much golden shadow material as dark. Do you hide your kindness for fear of being labelled as weak? Do you hide your joy for fear of being labelled as not serious enough?

Feel free to add some of the answers to your golden shadow questions if they are currently hidden traits.

At workshops I usually give participants about 10–15 minutes for steps 3 and 4.

If there is anything that you are absolutely unable to write down for fear of it being seen by another person, feel free to represent it through a symbol or acronym that only you know the meaning of. So if you are secretly into bondage, for example, write 'BF' on the inside of the mask to represent 'bondage fetish'. Then you can still get the benefits of releasing its energy into the mask without having a panic attack that your mum might see it!

Step 5

Once you have finished the inside of the mask, take some time to have a look at both sides and notice any correlations between the *persona* side and the shadow side. Do any qualities directly mirror each other or directly contradict each other?

How does it feel to hold the mask in your hands?

Take a moment to put the mask on your face. How does it feel?

Notice how your breathing is constricted by the mask. Notice how your true face is hidden by the mask. Notice how your ability to see is hindered by it.

Step 6

Stand in front of a mirror and hold the mask up at arm's length in front of your face with the *persona* side facing you.

Remind yourself that your *persona* is neither true nor false, it is just your preferred image of yourself. It is, at best, a pale photocopy of your true self and is nothing compared to who you really are.

Read out loud all the aspects of your *persona* and notice how each one makes you feel.

Step 7

Now flip the mask around so that the shadow side is facing you.

Remember, shame gains its power from being unspeakable, so to declare your shame out loud is to strip it of its power and liberate yourself from its stranglehold.

Read out loud all the aspects of your shadow side and notice how each one makes you feel.

Step 8

Finally, still holding the mask up in front of you, say each line three times out loud:

> *'I see you, my persona. I see you, my shadow.*
> *I am more than my persona.*
> *I am more than my shadow.'*

And then drop the mask. Literally drop it onto the floor and stand looking at your true face in the mirror.

Witness yourself with love and say three times out loud:

> *'I am the original face.'*

Dedication

And, as always, if it feels right to do so, dedicate the beneficial energy of this exercise to all beings, using the statement:

*'I dedicate the beneficial energy generated by
this exercise to the benefit of all beings.'*

You have just done what most people never do. You have just been brave enough to drop your mask and to see your original face. I honour that.

Step 9 (optional)

Only if and when you feel ready to do so, find a way to share your mask – both sides of it – with another person. This could be a close friend, or a therapist if you are currently seeing one. Speaking about what we present to others as well as what we hide from them is a very powerful way of befriending and releasing the contents of the mask. However, don't feel that you have to share your mask – it's totally optional.

And finally, in the Eleusinian Mysteries of ancient Greece you would be expected to make a confession to the community revealing your shadow before you could become an initiate, so I would like to offer you the chance to do something similar. If you like, you can email or DM me a photo of your mask (my email and socials can be found at www.charliemorley.com) and I will add it anonymously to the gallery on my Facebook page (Charlie Morley-Lucid Dreaming) called 'Shadow masks'. You will find literally hundreds of masks there already, in multiple languages, testament to the shared humanity of shadow work.

....

Real-Life Feedback

This exercise is not as simple as outside of the mask = good; inside of the mask = bad. It's about what we present to others and what we hide. For example, a woman on one of my courses wrote 'Bitch' on the outside of her mask, right across the forehead, because that is how she felt she had to present herself to the cut-throat male-dominated finance industry in which she worked.

And on the inside of the mask she wrote qualities such as 'girly' and 'silly/playful' that she felt she had to hide from others.

For many people at my workshops, this is the most powerful exercise they do there. One lady called Maki, a computer skills tutor who had struggled with self-love, told me:

> *'It was amazing. It clarified so much for me and really helped me. At the end, when I dropped the mask and saw my own face, I felt real love for myself – acceptance and self-love. It was brief, but I felt it. It was very powerful, and the feeling came back a few times in the following days too.'*

My friend Jenny, a child psychotherapist, found that the real breakthrough came when she shared her mask with her partner:

> *'My partner and I ended up doing the exercise together and then swapping masks at the end so that we could read each other's mask. It was so powerful "to have and to hold" the other's shadow.*
>
> *There were parts of my partner's mask which I identified with but hadn't yet named in my own shadow. This was super*

interesting, as the process of sharing their shadow actually illuminated unseen aspects of my own shadow. What an unexpected bonus!'

I've led thousands of people through that mask exercise in dozens of countries around the world, and each time I see the same stuff coming up. From hijab-wearing women at a workshop in Kuwait to TikTok teenagers at a conference in Estonia, we all seem to hide the same things: not only our shame and our fear, but also our deepest truths and our buried gold.

Once you start to do this work, you realize that everybody else is wearing a mask too. That's a great relief, because then you don't have to pretend as much. You can relax and be more open and honest with life. You can start to operate from a place of greater love and authenticity.

And the problem isn't actually the mask anyway – wearing a mask can be very helpful at times; if we are a parent, wearing the mask of the Father or Mother is often exactly what our child needs – the problem is the fact that we forget that we're wearing it and we mistake it for our real face.

RECAPS AND REFLECTIONS

✓ Shame perpetuates the disconnection that the addiction is trying to relieve.

✓ The *persona* is the side of ourselves that we show to others, our public face.

✓ The mask isn't the problem; the problem is that we forget we're wearing it.

» How did it feel to write your hidden traits on the inside of your mask?

» Are you willing to share your shadow mask with another person?

» To whom in your everyday life are you able to show your true face without any mask at all?

CHAPTER 10

BEFRIENDING THE SHADOW IN DREAMS AND NIGHTMARES

'The reason that we all dream so much is that the dreamer wants to remind us of the amount of shadow that we haven't yet absorbed.'

ROBERT BLY[1]

At the end of Part I we learned some exercises to help us connect to our dreams, and now at the end of Part II let's look at how these exercises can feed into something deeper.

Once you have established regular dream recall and started keeping a dream diary, you can begin recognizing and decoding the appearance of the shadow in your dreams.

We will be working from the basis that everything in a dream is in some way a reflection of your own psychology. From this perspective, your dark shadow becomes quite easy to recognize – it is anything or anyone in a dream that makes you feel afraid, disgusted, ashamed or annoyed. Anything in the dream that you would rather avoid, be it a situation or a person, might also be a reflection of your dark shadow, as of course is anything in the dream that reflects the contents of your bag or the inside of your mask.

And the golden shadow? You've guessed it: any person or situation in the dream that you admire, idolize or venerate. Dreams of well-loved celebrities, or of being a guest at an amazing party, or of flying, or doing things that make you feel alive, or meeting spiritual teachers – or maybe the people in your helium balloons – all carry a heavy dose of the golden shadow for most people.

Many people dream of having sex with celebrities, and celebrities that we admire often become golden shadow personifications when they appear in our dreams. Sex in dreams is often used as a symbol for unity and for bringing together that which is separate. So, if you dream of having sex with a certain celebrity, don't ignore it, but ask yourself, 'What qualities within me does this celebrity represent?' because it may be that those golden qualities are currently being unified within you.

Real-Life Feedback

A guy on one of the six-week shadow courses I ran felt that his shadow simply wasn't showing up in his dreams. I asked him if he'd noticed any changes in his dreams since he'd started the course and he said that he'd kept dreaming about the former British prime minister Theresa May. When I asked him what qualities she represented to him, he said, 'Steadiness, courage and strength.' As he spoke, his eyes lit up as he realized that those were three major traits on his projected golden shadow list!

Exercise: Decoding the Shadow in Dreams

· ·

As always, set your intention to remember your dreams as you fall asleep.

Upon awakening, recall and document your dreams in your dream diary. You don't have to write down every detail, but be sure to capture the main themes and feelings and the general narrative of the dream. You'll know what feels worth noting.

Then read through your dream and ask yourself the following five questions:

1. 'What are the dominant emotional themes of this dream?' For example, sadness, joy, searching, adventure.

2. 'Do any people, things or scenarios in the dream reflect aspects of my *dark* shadow? If so, which?'

3. 'Do any people, things or scenarios in the dream reflect aspects of my *golden* shadow? If so, which?'

4. 'Are there any aspects of my dream that may be personifications of my dark or golden shadow?' For example, celebrities, monsters, archetypal figures, animals, friends or enemies.

5. 'What do I think the dream wants to highlight for me?'

· ·

It takes time and practice to decode all the various shadow aspects in your dreams, but it's well worth doing. It's fascinating to see which aspects turn up and how they have been invoked or triggered by things you have suppressed, projected or acted out during the day.

To make a conscious effort to get in touch with the feeling of a dream (rather than just recalling its content) is to spend time hanging out with your unconscious, paying homage to its offerings and familiarizing yourself with your shadow.

Once you know what to look for, you'll soon find your shadow playing a central role (or at least making a cameo appearance) in many of your dreams. This is a good sign, as it shows that the shadow is ready to reveal itself and wants to be integrated.

Reframing Nightmares

'With genuine self-acceptance and a sense of humour we can uncover even the darkest inner monsters with love.'
ROB PREECE[2]

Nightmares are one of the most visceral encounters with our shadow that many of us will ever experience, and so by reframing our perception of them we can begin to befriend their content.

Many of us pathologize our nightmares as symptoms of a broken mind and so naturally try to get rid of them. In fact, nightmares are not only ways to meet our shadow, but often calls for attention from a mind that is trying to make itself heard.

Over the past 15 years I've worked with thousands of nightmare sufferers, including armed forces veterans, victims of childhood abuse and even survivors of terrorist attacks. What I've noticed is that for many of these people, the deepest healing has come from a shift of perspective concerning what nightmares actually are. Once they recognize that they are a call for help rather than an attack by the unconscious, the road to healing opens up before them.

A Dream That Is Shouting

Nightmares don't mean to hurt us, they mean to grab our attention. A nightmare is simply a dream that is shouting. It is shouting, 'Hey, look at this! Deal with this! This shadow needs attention!'

Dr Justin Havens, a psychological therapist who conducted his PhD research into the PTSD nightmares of military veterans, agrees, saying, 'When bad things happen, we are supposed to dream about them, because the nightmare is highlighting a problematic aspect such as unresolved emotional distress that needs to be integrated.'[3]

Just as physical pain is used by our brain to tell us to attend to a wounded part of our body, so nightmares are used by our unconscious mind to make us attend to a wounded part of our psyche. A nightmare isn't shouting in order to scare us but to help us. And so, if we want to reduce the frequency of our nightmares, we need to do everything we can to tell our unconscious mind, 'Okay, okay! I'm listening. No need to shout so loud!'

This can be done by writing our nightmares down, drawing pictures of them or discussing them with a therapist or trusted friend. Essentially, we want to do everything we can to show the unconscious mind that we hear it loud and clear. This is the opposite of the New Age delusion that claims that to write a nightmare down or to recount it out loud might serve to 'manifest it into reality'.

This kind of spiritual bypassing is not only complete bullshit, but may also be a dangerous slide into denial and suppression, which may create even more shadow content. In fact, through the act of bearing witness to a nightmare, we can release the underlying emotional charge or trauma that is creating it and allow it to be integrated into our psycho-physical system.

Signs of a Healing Mind

Essentially, our mind uses nightmares to treat and heal its wounds. If we cut our arm, our body bleeds and then sends coagulates and white blood cells to form a protective layer over the wound to prevent any further damage. This allows the healing process to continue below the surface. If this didn't happen, we might end up with sepsis or gangrene from every minor wound. A nightmare works in a similar way; just like a scab, it's a manifestation of the healing process, in this case one used by the mind to regulate emotions and integrate traumatic experiences.

Also, just as picking at a scab can lead to further bleeding, if we pick at or dwell on our nightmares too much, this can slow up the healing process. It's all about balance.

Of course, I'm not suggesting that we *have* to have nightmares in order to heal, but if trauma remains unwitnessed and thus unintegrated, our mind's natural self-healing mechanism will take things into its own hands.

There is science to back this up too. Studies led by the brilliant Dr Rosalind Cartwright at Rush University in Chicago looking at the effects of depression caused by trauma showed that 'only patients who were expressly dreaming about the painful experiences' around the time of them actually happening became clinically free of their depression. Those who were dreaming, but not actually dreaming about their emotionally painful or traumatic experiences, showed no such improvement. Healing was predicated on 'dreaming about the emotional themes and sentiments of the waking state trauma'.[4]

Nightmares as an Evolutionary Tool

Whereas our first two reframes explain how nightmares help to integrate past traumas, our third one explains how they may be used to help us survive future ones too. One of the key reasons why we came to be the dominant species was not only our ability to dream, and thus explore future actions, but more specifically, it was our ability to have nightmares. Professor Antti Revonsuo, a Finnish scientist who created the threat simulation theory of dreaming, believes that REM (rapid eye movement) dreaming is 'an ancient biological defence mechanism evolutionarily selected for its capacity to repeatedly simulate threatening events'.[5]

Imagine two prehistoric women sharing a cave. One of them has frequent nightmares about sabre-toothed tigers and how to fight them, run from them or hide from them, while the other one has peaceful dreams. If they were to meet a sabre-toothed tiger in waking life, which would be better placed to survive and pass on her genes?

Professor Revonsuo concludes, 'Nightmares force us to go through simulated threatening events so that in the waking world we are more prepared to survive them.'[6] Proof again that nightmares can actually be good for us.

As someone who has suffered with terrible nightmares in the past, I know that even though they are trying to help, they are still very unpleasant and uncomfortable experiences. So let's look at a great exercise for anyone suffering from the fear that nightmares can often unwittingly cause.

Exercise: The Circle of Protectors

Shadow work isn't meant to be scary, but sometimes our ego can make it feel as though it is, especially if we're currently working with nightmares too. So, if ever you feel a bit scared or anxious before sleep, this exercise is what you need.

It is a visualization practice in which you imagine a gathering of protectors around you, fearlessly supporting your shadow work and standing guard over you as you sleep.

This exercise was inspired by an ancient practice within the indigenous Tibetan lineage of Bön and it's particularly helpful for anyone working with nightmares, night terrors or pre-sleep anxiety. It's one of the favourite techniques when I work with groups who are experiencing PTSD trauma nightmares.

The original Tibetan teachings say that if you are feeling scared or anxious before you sleep, you should turn your sleeping area into a sacred protected space by imagining that you are surrounded by enlightened beings and *dakinis*, female embodiments of awakening, who remain 'like mothers watching over a child or guardians surrounding a king or queen'.[7]

But who should *you* visualize as your protectors? Anyone or anything who offers you a feeling of love, safety, allegiance and protection. Your protectors can be living or dead, real or unreal, known or unknown. Personally, I might imagine Lama Yeshe Rinpoche (my Buddhist teacher), my deceased mum (nobody had my back like she did), Rob Nairn (my mentor) and my little sausage dog, Waffles (she is as brave as a wolf and would do anything to protect me), in the four cardinal directions (north, south, east and west) and then fill the gaps with other imagined protectors.

Some people I've taught this practice to fall asleep imagining a buffalo, Jesus, a ball of white light and Gandalf, the wizard from *The Lord of the Rings*, standing guard. Be creative. There are no rules for this – you can't get it wrong.

I find that invoking an imagined gathering of my protectors is a powerful preparation, not only for sleep but also for whichever shadow work exercise I am about to do, so don't feel limited to bedtime when engaging this technique.

For this practice, you can follow the guided audio meditation track that I've made at www.charliemorley.com/resources or you can guide yourself through the following steps:

–   Decide which protectors you're going to invoke.

–   Lying in bed before sleep, close your eyes and allow yourself to relax into the shallows of the hypnagogic state.

–   Imagine your first protector standing or sitting near your head. You don't have to see them clearly, just know that they're there, watching over you, protecting you, holding you in their love.

–   Next, imagine your second protector sitting or standing by your feet. Your second protector is watching over you with love. Feel the power of their protection.

–   Now, imagine your third protector on your left-hand side. Feel their love, their safety beaming down to you. You now have protectors by your head, your feet and your left-hand side. You don't have to see them clearly, just know that they're there.

–   And now imagine your fourth protector sitting or standing by your right-hand side, watching over you and exuding a feeling of safety, of love.

–   Take a moment to feel the love, the safety and the protection your protectors are offering you. You're surrounded by protection. You're surrounded by love.

–   And finally, fill in the gaps between the protectors. Again, you could do this with people or animals or balls of light, crystals, fire, weapons, stars, galaxies, fairy lights... Whatever you choose, fill in the gaps between each of the four primary protectors, completing your circle of protectors.

– Hold that visualization for as long as you can, then let it fade, let it slip from your mind's eye as you drift through the hypnagogic state and into sleep, knowing you are protected.

. . . .

THE SCIENCE OF SLEEP PARALYSIS

No chapter on nightmares and the shadow would be complete without looking at sleep paralysis, the phenomenon of partially waking from sleep but the body remaining paralysed.

For many people, this is a terrifying experience in which hallucinatory images and sounds may lead them to believe that demons are trying to possess them or that there are dark forces in the bedroom.

Thankfully, sleep paralysis has now been scientifically explained, which helps to put the demonic myths of the past to bed. So, what is actually happening from a scientific point of view?

Sleep paralysis is caused by one of the three REM sleep systems (the things that happen when we enter REM dreaming sleep), muscular paralysis, staying engaged when the other two, sensory blockade and cortical activation, have been disengaged, meaning that while our brain has partially woken up and our senses are taking in partial input, our physical body cannot move.

Due to our brain's momentary engagement in both the dream state and waking state, hallucinatory images may be superimposed over our normal field of vision, and there are often loud audio hallucinations too. The fear that this altered state generates can also lead to hyperventilation, and in turn a feeling of weight on the chest. No wonder that in earlier times demonic visitation often seemed to be the best explanation.

If you want to break free from sleep paralysis, often the best course of action is to actively relax and exhale (or imagine exhaling) through your front teeth, making a sound similar to letting air out of a tyre. This relaxation of the respiratory system will help to disengage the paralysis mechanism.

Healing Nightmares through Lucid Dreaming

Once you've reframed your view of nightmares, you might feel ready to intentionally become conscious within them and learn how to transform them through the practice of lucid dreaming.

If you've ever had a dream in which you've realized, *Oh wow, I'm dreaming! I'm in a dream right now, I can decide what to do!*, that was a lucid dream.

In a lucid dream we haven't woken up – in fact, we're still sound asleep – but part of our brain has reactivated allowing us to experience the dream state consciously and to direct the dream at will.

Although some people can lucid dream naturally, my job for the past 15 years has been teaching people how to do it. I run workshops and have written books on the subject; in fact, the first iteration of this book, *Dreaming Through Darkness*, has several chapters on shadow work through lucid dreaming.

Lucid dreaming is without doubt one of the most powerful ways to integrate nightmares and heal trauma. In June 2023 the peer-reviewed journal *Traumatology* published the results of a scientific study that I facilitated with the Institute of Noetic Sciences in California.[8] It was a pilot study with 55 participants, all of whom had chronic post-traumatic stress disorder and had used lucid dreaming to treat not just their nightmares, but also their waking-state symptoms.

Over six days the participants received 22 hours of lucid dream tuition delivered via Zoom and were taught not only how to lucid dream but specifically how to use lucid dreaming to transform their nightmares and integrate their trauma.

The results of the study were really quite amazing, with the majority of participants experiencing 'a remarkable decrease in PTSD symptoms'[9] as well as a huge drop in nightmare frequency within just one week, using lucid dreaming alone. In fact, by the end of the sixth day of the study over 85 per cent of the participants reported such a massive drop in waking-state trauma symptoms that they were no longer classified as having post-traumatic stress disorder. The lead scientist of the study, Dr Garret Yount, called these results 'highly significant and truly remarkable'.[10] Check out the following graph.

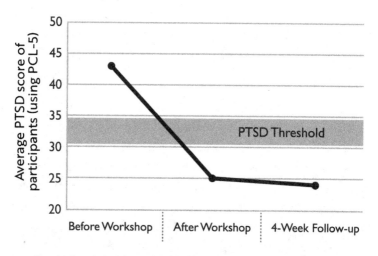

Graph showing reduction of PTSD symptoms after participants attended a lucid dreaming healing workshop.

Although this was just a 55-person pilot study, we have since conducted a 100-person randomized control study, which followed the same protocol and in which we were able to replicate similar results again under control conditions. This follow-up study will be published in summer 2025.

So, both the pilot study and the 100-person randomized control study show without doubt that lucid dreaming may be one of the most effective treatments for post-traumatic stress disorder currently available. It's non-invasive, non-addictive, non-medical plus it's free and you literally do it in your sleep.

With PTSD and trauma being two of the biggest contributors to many people's shadow content, we can see how learning to lucid dream is a brilliant tool for shadow workers to have. We won't be exploring how to lucid dream here, but for those who do want to learn how to do it, visit my website (*see p.232*) and check out my books, workshops and online courses.

RECAPS AND REFLECTIONS

✓ A nightmare is simply a dream that is shouting.

✓ The mind uses nightmares to treat and heal its wounds.

✓ Sleep paralysis is (almost certainly) not a demonic visitation, so try to chill and breathe out a long exhalation.

✓ Lucid dreaming is one of the most powerful interventions for PTSD currently available.

» Have you ever had a celebrity sex dream, and if so, what golden qualities might that person represent for you?

» What do your nightmares tell you about the content of your shadow?

» Who were your protectors in the 'Circle of Protectors' exercise?

PART III

TRANSFORMING THE SHADOW

'To own one's shadow is the purpose of life. A full-bodied embracing of our own humanity.'

ROBERT A. JOHNSON[1]

So far we've met and befriended our shadow. Now we'll learn how to transform its energy alchemically through a set of practices that may ask us to rethink our relationship with ourselves in quite revolutionary ways.

You will be asked to explore the often fertile mud of your past pain, heal your relationship with your parents, make a pilgrimage back to the lands of your ancestors, own your sexual story and confront your own mortality. These practices may evoke quite powerful responses within you, so it is essential that you don't force anything here.

Before embarking on each exercise in this part, I encourage you to pause for a few minutes and ask yourself, 'Is this the right time for me to engage in this process? Do I feel that it's being kind to myself to address this at this time? Do I feel sufficiently confident and supported, both spiritually and/or emotionally, in exploring this part of myself?'

Breathe deeply, open your heart and prepare yourself. Now is the time to transform your shadow. To let a lotus rise from the mud.

CHAPTER 11

NO MUD, NO LOTUS

*'Most people are afraid of suffering. But
suffering is a kind of mud to help the
lotus flower of happiness grow.'*

Thích Nhất Hạnh[1]

In almost all schools of Eastern mysticism the lotus flower is
seen as a symbol of our innate enlightened potential. The
reason for this stems from how the lotus grows.

To grow a lotus, you need mud. Lotus seeds germinate most
readily in the deep sludge at the bottom of ponds. When they
sprout, they are naturally attracted to sunlight and instinctively
reach up to it, eventually blossoming on the surface of the water,
untainted by the mud from whence they came, pristine, perfect
and beautiful.

You cannot grow a lotus flower in clean water or in a crystal vase;
it requires the mud of the pond, and the muddy pond is like our
shadowy mind. All the dark, traumatic, unloved aspects of both
our mind and our life form the fertile mud in which the lotus

of our true potential can grow. Without the mud, there can be no lotus.

The first time I came across this concept, I was shocked to learn that rather than getting rid of my muddy, shadowy, seemingly 'negative' mind-states, I could *actively use* them for spiritual growth.

It's been said that 'suffering and awakening form from a single weather-system'[2] and so we can be glad of our pain, for it opens our heart. This is nice advice, but when we are knee-deep in the mud of our own suffering, it sucks, and it can be difficult to imagine a lotus growing there.

With time, though, we often come to realize that the pain that we've experienced in our life has made us who we are, and that if it hadn't been for that painful loss, heartbreak, illness or breakdown, we wouldn't have encountered the amazing life changes or opportunities that these led to. There is a Tibetan saying: 'Just as a bonfire in a strong wind isn't blown out but blazes even brighter, so our mind can be strengthened by the difficult situations we encounter.'

This isn't about spiritual bypassing and 'looking on the bright side', but simply about acknowledging how the mud of suffering can often lead to psychological or spiritual growth. The break-up that led to you finding your true self, the brush with death that made you wake up to life, the redundancy that allowed you to explore your passion – all of these are examples of 'no mud, no lotus'.

To become a shadow worker is to become the gardener of our own mind, acknowledging that the trauma, fear and shame that create our shadow aren't things to get rid of, they create the fertile mud from which grows the lotus of our true self.

Exercise: Finding the Lotus in the Mud

This exercise, originally inspired by my friend and mindfulness teacher Fay Adams, asks you to find moments in your life when the mud of suffering led to the lotus of new growth, happiness, opportunity or insight.

When I first did this exercise, I thought back to the panic attacks that led me to find Buddhist meditation, the nightmares of my teens that led me to lucid dreaming and the heartbreak of my mid-thirties that led me finally to face myself.

At workshops people have shared how losing their job led them to the career they had always dreamed of, how mental breakdown led them to the spiritual path and how illness was the wake-up call that led to living a fuller life.

So I ask you, when in *your* life has the mud of suffering led to the blossoming of your lotus?

— Take a moment to come into an awareness of your breath. Just notice when you are breathing in and notice when you are breathing out.

— Notice three breaths before you begin.

— Using the diagram on the following page or making your own, write on the mud section any times of suffering that you now see led to psychological or spiritual growth. Even if you can only think of one or two examples, that's fine.

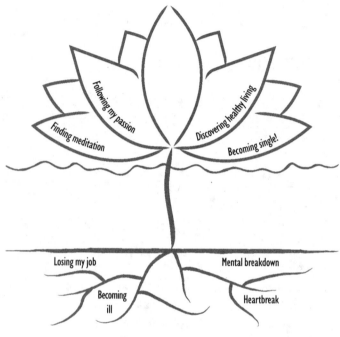

Create your own lotus

— Now, write onto the lotus petals the beneficial things that blossomed from each of the experiences that you wrote in the mud section – for example, a new perspective on life, freedom from a toxic relationship, the opportunity to follow your passion.

— Take a moment to think back to what happened and to appreciate and perhaps even to send gratitude to the people or situations that created the mud.

– And if it feels right to do so, dedicate the beneficial energy of this exercise to all beings, using the statement:

'I dedicate the beneficial energy generated by this exercise to the benefit of all beings.'

....

THE SCIENCE OF NO MUD, NO LOTUS

The 'no mud, no lotus' concept has verification from mainstream psychology. Most of us have heard about PTSD, but far fewer have heard about PTG. Post-Traumatic Growth is the phenomenon of positive change coming about through the experience of trauma and adversity. Many people find that traumatic experiences can actually lead to beneficial change in their lives. Not all people by any means, but more than half of all trauma survivors actually report positive change.[3]

A 2009 *British Journal of Health Psychology* article reviewing the past 20 years of studies into PTG reported:

'The studies consistently found that their respondents had a new appreciation of life, calling it a "gift", and that they were "thankful" that they had been touched by such life-altering illnesses or events.'[4]

Many trauma survivors can 'arrive at an even higher level of psychological and emotional functioning than before the adversity',[5] but crucially this usually happens *after* 'the acute period of depression, anxiety or nightmares caused by the trauma', so we do still have to go through the mud.

Researchers commented how 'people said that despite the physical pain they suffered [and] the daily struggles they faced, their lives were unquestionably better... than before their traumatic experiences. Trauma sent them on a path they never would have found otherwise.'[6]

So often we see ourselves as lonely victims among strangers who don't know our pain. But everyone has been through pain and suffering. And everyone is a lotus ready to bloom. Imagine if we could take time to really witness the mud that another person has been through as well as the lotus of awakening that is within them.

Can we be willing to sit in the mud with another person and not try to pull them out? Can we be confident enough just to sit with them, in the mud, in the shit, together, just being with them without trying to change them or the situation? If we can, then that is often the greatest gift we can give them.

Exercise: Witnessing the Lotus

This exercise builds on the last one and asks you to see the lotus and the mud in another person. It is inspired by an eye-gazing technique taught to me by my friend, the philosopher Tim Freke (yup, that's his real name), and it explores vulnerability, projection, empathy and the golden shadow.

Along with the two-faced mask exercise (see p.100), this is a firm favourite with participants at my workshops, and one young journalist even said it was one of the most powerful compassion exercises he had ever done. It's one of my personal favourites too, so I implore you not to skip it just because it requires a partner. Find someone, anyone, even a stranger if you like, but be sure to do this exercise.

Because you and your partner will each have your eyes closed at different times, it is best done as a guided meditation. A version can be found set to music and guided by my voice on my website (www.charliemorley.com/shadowexercises) under the title 'Witnessing the Lotus.' Or you can record your own version following the steps below.

Step 1

Sit opposite your partner. Decide who is person A and who is person B.

Person A and person B close your eyes. Take a moment to breathe and become aware of your body being supported unconditionally by the chair or cushion beneath you.

Your intention for this exercise is to bear witness to your partner with compassionate awareness. To see them fully and completely. To witness both their mud and their lotus.

Step 2

And now, person A, open your eyes. Take a moment to bear witness to your partner. Take a moment to recognize the mud of their struggle. Just like you, they have known pain. Just like you, they have made mistakes. Just like you, they have dark shadow material. And just like you, they are trying their best. Hold them in your awareness for the next few moments.

And now, person A, close your eyes, and person B, open your eyes. Person B, take a moment to bear witness to your partner. Take a moment to recognize the mud of their struggle. Just like you, they have known pain. Just like you, they have made mistakes. Just like you, they have dark shadow material. Just like you, they are trying their best. Hold them in your awareness for the next few moments.

Now, person B, close your eyes, and person A, open your eyes. Person A, take a moment to bear witness to your partner. Take a moment to recognize the lotus of their true potential, their divine light, their hidden gold. Just like you, they have enlightened potential. Just like you, they have inner gold. They are a lotus ready to bloom. Hold them in your awareness for the next few moments.

Now, person A, close your eyes, and person B, open your eyes. Person B, take a moment to bear witness to your partner. Take a moment to recognize the lotus of their true potential, their divine light, their hidden gold. Just like you, they have enlightened potential. Just like you, they have inner gold. They are a lotus ready to bloom. Hold them in your awareness for the next few moments.

Step 3

Person A, keep your eyes closed, and person B, close your eyes too.

Step 4

Now that you have seen each other's mud and lotus, prepare to bear witness to the whole person, to see their original face with compassionate awareness.

Person A and person B, open your eyes.

Look into each other's eyes and really see the person. See beyond their mask, see beyond their shadow, see their original face.

Witness their humanity. You are dreamers in the same dream, both wanting love and both trying your best, both sleeping buddhas slowly awakening to your full potential. Look into their eyes and witness the power of their humanity.

Hold each other's gaze for the next few moments, or even minutes if you can.

Step 5

Then find a way to thank your partner and spend some time sharing your experience. Ask each other:

– 'How was it to be witnessed with your eyes closed?'

– 'How was it to see me when I couldn't see you?'

– 'What did it feel like when we both opened our eyes and saw each other?'

Dedication

Take a moment to dedicate the beneficial energy that you have just generated to all living beings, using the statement:

> *'I dedicate the beneficial energy generated by this exercise to the benefit of all beings.'*

RECAPS AND REFLECTIONS

✓ The mud of our suffering can fertilize the seeds of psychological growth.

✓ Just as a bonfire in a strong wind isn't blown out but blazes even brighter, so your mind can be strengthened by the difficult situations you encounter.

✓ PTG is for real. Not in all cases by any means, but in about 50 per cent of cases trauma survivors actually report positive change after recovery.

» Do you think you have ever experienced any PTG?

» What did you learn from doing the 'No mud, no lotus' exercise?

» How was the eye-gazing for you?

CHAPTER 12

HEALING THE PARENTAL SHADOW

*'If you think you're enlightened go
spend a week with your parents.'*

BABA RAM DASS (ATTRIBUTED)[1]

In many ways, our shadow is not only the product of who we are but also of who we have come from, and so until we acknowledge and accept that, our unhelpful shadow patterns may well keep recurring.

My interest in ancestral shadow work was sparked by a comment from my friend Stephen Victor, who is an esteemed life coach with particular expertise in family constellation work. He said that the ancestral shadow held the key to integrating the personal one and explained why it was so important to integrate it:

'If you cut your foot on a large nail, you would rightly take action to heal it. Failing to do so imperils your foot, or life.

Believe it or not, failing to heal the ancestral shadow may cost you life and limb too, because so often the root cause of many of our difficulties lies in the energy lines of those who came before us. Freeing ourselves from this conditioning is imperative if we're to live the lives awaiting us.[2]

Of course, this doesn't mean that we should ascribe blame to our ancestral line or reject responsibility for who we are, simply that we should be aware that the ability to respond to our current challenges may be found in our familial past as much as in our present.

And with that in mind, I set out to integrate the energy of my ancestors. I began with my nearest ones: my mum and dad.

In the Shadows of Our Parents

As part of the exercise opposite, I ask you to write a letter to one of your parents. In his reply to that letter, my dad told me:

'The truth is no one tells you how to be a good parent. You rely on human instinct and memories of your own childhood – both good and bad. In my case, having grown up without a father, having sons meant much of the time I was all at sea...'

It took a long time for my dad and me to reach the level of openness and authenticity that those words reveal, but the first vital step along the way was when he finally told me his story...

Steve Biddulph, author of the brilliant book *Manhood*, believes that 'without understanding our fathers and knowing them well, we cannot decide what we want to take and what we want to leave of their legacy'[3] and so we inherit their shadow traits by default. He believes that until we come to terms with them, they will haunt us from the inside. Although Biddulph is talking specifically about our father's story, I believe that this can be applied to our mother's story too.

If we can come to know our parents' stories, we can come to understand why they are the way they are and move our relationship into empathy and understanding. At the same time we can start to become aware of the shadow traits we may have inherited from them. Doing so enables us to stop unconsciously playing them out or, even worse, passing them on to our own children.

Even if one (or both) of your parents was absent, abusive, lost or even dead before you met them, you have a choice: to come to terms with the legacy that they handed to you or to share your life with the ghost of their shadow.

My friend Lama Choyin Rangdrol, a brilliant African-American Buddhist lama, once told me, 'It's important to identify your parents' demons so you can defend yourself from making them your own. Your parents' demons are not your own. With awareness and practice, you can allow yourself to escape their bad habits. Then you are free.'[4]

Exercise: Healing the Parental Shadow

This exercise asks you to spend time alone with your father or mother and to have a series of conversations in which you seek to understand their life, their reasons for being, their successes and their failures.

You are encouraged to travel back into their past with them, learn about who they were before they were your parent and learn how they became the person they were when they co-created you.

If your father or mother is dead, or you have lost all contact with them, you can still do a version of this exercise and I will explain how later (see p.143).

The aim of this exercise is to humanize your father or mother, to empathize with their role as a person rather than solely as your parent and compassionately to bear witness to their story as a way of helping them integrate their own shadow while you integrate your parental one.

I wasn't close to my dad growing up, but when I did this exercise with him in my early thirties, it totally changed our relationship. He took me back to the place in north London where he had grown up. He showed me where he had gone to school and the street that he had grown up on. He opened up about what he had been like as a child and how his teenage years had been. I realized afterwards that it was the longest one-on-one conversation we had ever had. When had I ever spoken to my dad for five hours straight before?

I will outline the complete process, but please see it simply as a template of possibility, as I am aware that some parents may be totally unwilling to engage with certain parts of this process. Please feel free to do as much or as little of it as possible, but do try and ask all of the questions at least.

Step 1

Ideally, arrange to spend a day or afternoon with either your father or mother, journeying back into their past with them as the tour guide. You don't have to mention shadow integration or anything like that. Just let them know that this is not an invitation to argue, that you are not coming armed with old resentments and that your only aim is to hear their story.

If you can, make a real-life journey back to the place of their birth or where they grew up or went to school. Ask them to show you around and to guide you back into their history. If this is too much, simply arrange to go for a long drive or a walk with them, alone and undisturbed.

Step 2

Once you are alone, start to ask them about the story of their life. Defensiveness may be the 'go to' response from some parents, so take it slowly.

Below are 15 of the questions that I suggest you ask them, but of course feel free to change them or to add your own.

Whatever they answer, just allow them to speak, and if they don't want to answer a question, just let it go or maybe give your own answer as a way of showing them that you are ready to share openly too.

Try not to ask these questions as if you are interrogating your parent; ask them with kindness and curiosity.

1. 'What were you like as a child?'

2. 'How was your upbringing?'

3. 'What was your relationship like with your father and mother?'

4. 'What were you scared of as a child?'

5. 'Do you remember your first kiss?'

6. 'What was your first job?'

7. 'Where did you live when you first left home?'

8. 'What did you dream of doing with your life?'

9. 'How did you feel when you first became a parent?'

10. 'What was going on in your life when I was born?'

11. 'What's your greatest fear?'

12. 'What things in life have you been most ashamed of?'

13. 'What parts of yourself do you struggle to love?'

14. 'What things in life bring out the best in you?'

15. 'What would you have liked to have done with your life if you hadn't become a parent?

You can spread the questions out over the day if you like or you can ask them all in one sitting. It's up to you. The answers to these questions led me to ask dozens of others too, but these are a pretty good starting-point. They are just suggestions, though, and if your parent is unwilling to answer any, that's totally fine. All you can do is ask.

The exercise ends whenever you feel that they have answered all that they can or whenever the day naturally comes to an end.

Step 3

Within a few days, write them an email or letter of thanks (they will have been waiting), not just for the day you spent together but for anything else you might want to thank them for. Now is the perfect time.

You don't have to forget their failures or forgive them for their wrongs, but do write to them, letting them know that you bear witness to their story and are grateful to them for sharing it.

Don't expect a reply, but if they do reply, then feel free to continue the dialogue.

Once you have done this exercise with one parent, you may like to do it with your other parent, too, but keep the experiences separate.

For Parents Who Have Passed

If your father or mother is dead, or you have lost all contact with them, you can still do a version of this exercise either by making a pilgrimage back to their home and significant places in their life and/or through conversations with family members who remember them, using photos if you wish.

Ask the questions in Step 2 to those who knew them before you were born and write down or record their answers.

Then write your parent a letter of thanks, acknowledging what you have learned about them from the questions, and then burn it as a way of ritually sending it to them and of gaining closure over the process.

You might also take the letter-writing as an opportunity to say what needed to be said when you were younger or to have the conversation with them that you wished you could have had before they died. Be sure not to blame, though; instead, use the awareness of their shadow side that you have gained through the questions to try to understand (not condone, but understand) their behaviours.

•••

I encourage anybody with a fractured parental relationship to do this exercise. I found it to be a powerful practice that was instrumental in healing the wounded relationship that I had with my father. Sitting on the train back home, I realized that I'd learned more about him in those five hours than I had in the previous 33 years. I felt that I now knew some of his story and already I felt greater empathy, greater respect and greater love for him, not just as my father, but as a man.

Real-Life Feedback

A 60-year-old man from Australia emailed to tell me that he had done this exercise with his 83-year-old mother. He told me that they had had a very uneasy relationship since childhood and had been estranged for many years.

They had never really spoken of much beyond surface-level things, but she was open to doing the exercise and they spent hours discussing her youth and the life she had lived before she had given birth to him. She told him everything about her teenage years and the dramas of her youth. She even told him for the first time how she had sought an abortion, then hadn't gone through with it.

He told me:

> 'The thing about this exercise with my mother wasn't that she told me anything I didn't already know. I'd sort of heard the story from other people, so it wasn't so much that I learned new things. The important thing was that my mother was willing to tell me that story, her story. The breakthrough was that finally I heard it from her.
>
> Since then, our conversations have gone back pretty much to how they always used to be. But of course both of us remember the conversation and always will do.'

Becoming the Parent We Needed

So much of integrating the shadow is about learning how to reparent ourselves. Reparenting is the act of giving yourself what you didn't receive as a child.

We have all had the experience of not being loved in the way we needed to be loved by our parents or primary caregivers, and the wounds inflicted by a parent on an adult child can cut just as deep as those inflicted in childhood, but whenever it has happened, it's never too late to reparent ourselves and to heal the wounds of our inner child.

Healing the Inner Child

There is an energy inside us that always connects us to childhood. It's called the inner child.

Dr Charles Whitfield, author of *Healing the Child Within*, tells us that the concept of the inner child has been around for over 2,000 years, but in the West it was Carl Jung who popularized it as the archetypal representation of our childhood experiences (both harmful and helpful).[5]

We all have an inner child, a part of ourselves connected to both our past childhood experiences and our present childlike energy, or lack of it. Our inner child is the current expression of our connection to playfulness, joy and innocence and also the summation of all of our actual childhood experiences and the unmet needs of the idealized child that we hoped we might be.

Due to it being the dominant internal archetype of our childhood, when traumatic childhood experiences negatively affect us, it is our inner child that may carry these wounds.

A wounded inner child leads not only to an inability to connect fully to our inner joy, but also to acting out childhood patterns in our adult life. Most of us would agree that childhood experiences leave an almost indelible mark on the psyche and, although often seemingly forgotten, still impact us today.

The psychotherapist David Richo, PhD, believes that healing the inner child is essential for our psychological health and wellbeing and that to step fully into adulthood, we must befriend, heal and empower our inner child.

If only we could take a time machine back to our childhood and be there to tell our wounded younger self, 'It's okay, it's not your fault,' or 'You haven't done anything wrong, you are still loved deeply, they just can't live with each other any more,' or whatever it was that we so desperately needed to hear.

Although we may not have a time machine, there are certain practices that allow us to do this. The best way to communicate with our inner child is through things that circumvent the conscious mind, such as imagination, art and creative writing.

The following exercise asks you to use all three to communicate with that part of yourself that is forever connected to both your past childhood experiences and your present childlike energy. It is a kind of retroactive healing exercise: you will offer healing in the present to the part of yourself that was wounded in the past.

Exercise: Letter to Your Inner Child

As an act of reparenting, I invite you to write a letter to your inner child and draw them a picture too. The letter will be written from yourself as an adult to yourself as a child of around seven to 10 years old. (If you would prefer to use a different age, older or younger, then that's fine too.)

This is your chance to acknowledge your inner child, to let them know that you remember them and, crucially, to give them the words of affirmation that you wish you had heard during childhood.

It is a brilliant way to start the reparenting process.

Step 1

Using the example below as inspiration, write a letter to your inner child, including:

- calling them by the name that you would want to be called as a child (maybe a nickname you liked or wished you had been called)

- information about who you are now and how you spend your life

- the acknowledgement that you wished you could have received

Offer them words of encouragement as you tell them that you know what happened to them and that it wasn't their fault.

Tell them what you wanted and needed to hear as a child but didn't (I advise making three key points at least).

Tell them what you are currently doing or intend to do to reconnect with them.

And finally, thank them.

Here is my letter as an example (note the simple language and the playful tone):

Dear Chuck,

My name is Charlie and I am 40 years old now...

I am you, but the grown-up version of you.

I know that I haven't been in touch much recently, but I want to change that from now on please, Chuck.

I – we, both of us – live in London now with our little sausage dog, who is called Waffles, and our girlfriend, who is called Chloe. She has a big fluffy dog called Bao. Waffles is very brave, but she is tiny, and Bao is very big and fluffy, but he's a bit of a scaredy cat!

For our job, we help people with their sleep and dreams and with being happier by being brave and not so worried about the things they hide.

We also help army people to get better when they have nightmares after scary battles. Our life is really fun and not boring.

I want to tell you three important things, Chuck.

I want you to know that you are a very good little boy and that when Daddy blames you for things, it isn't because he doesn't love you, it's because he's sad and angry with himself. I know you are a bit naughty sometimes, but you are never mean, and most of the time you're just trying to make people laugh.

The reason that you find classes at school a bit tricky is because you are dyslexic. That means that your brain works differently from the brains of other people. You are not stupid, you are very clever, and when Mummy finds out that you are dyslexic, you get special help and then you start to enjoy school much more!

I want you to know that your brother loves you too and that when you grow up, you are very good friends. Your funny loud energy is sometimes a bit scary for him, because he is a bit shy, and quieter than you, and that's why he says hurtful things to you. This isn't your fault, though, and he doesn't really mean it anyway.

With all these things – your daddy, your brother and your struggles at school – I want to tell you that it isn't your fault, you are a good little boy and people love you so much! And when you grow up, you are very good friends with your brother and your daddy, and you are so good at school that you even end up writing whole entire books!

Oh, and I have started surfing again these past few years because I know how you love to do that, and I'm trying to do fewer boring things and to have more fun too. Ever since we were a teenager, we've been doing lots of martial arts like in Karate Kid and we even have a black belt like Mr Miyagi now, so we can protect people and not be scared of bullies.

I am always here with you, Chuck, and I love you so much, just like your mummy and daddy do.

Lots of love,

Charlie (you as a grown-up)

Step 2

Along with the letter, draw a picture for your inner child as an offering to them. It could be a picture of you as an adult with your significant others or it could be a picture of whatever your favourite animal was as a child. Be creative, you can't get it wrong: as a little child, what would you like a picture of?

Step 3

Sit in front of a mirror with a photo of yourself as a child stuck onto the mirror so that you can see both your reflection and the photo.

Read the letter out loud to the photo of yourself stuck on the mirror.

Step 4

Finally, burn the letter and the drawing as a way of symbolically sending it to your inner child.

....

RECAPS AND REFLECTIONS

✓   Your parents' demons are not your own.

✓   It is never too late to be the parent that you needed.

✓   We experience the wounded inner child whenever we act in a child*ish* way and the healthy inner child whenever we act in a child*like* way.

»   Are you able to set a date to do the 'Healing the Parental Shadow' exercise?

»   How did it feel to write the letter to your inner child?

»   What drawing did you create for your inner child and why?

»   As Keila Shaheen asks in *The Shadow Work Journal*, 'What activities can you do as an adult to fuel your inner child?'[6]

CHAPTER 13

INTEGRATING THE ANCESTRAL SHADOW

*'We're all ghosts. We all carry, inside us,
the people who came before us.'*

LIAM CALLANAN[1]

The integration of our ancestral shadow frees up huge amounts of the psychic energy that is tied up in our family line. We loosen the chains that shackle us to our bloodline and make conscious the ancestral shadow patterns that may have been playing out in our life. Freeing ourselves from these patterns allows us to move forward without the burden of our ancestral conditioning.

By tracing back our family line, we can compassionately witness the dark shadows of our ancestors and pay homage to their golden potential by celebrating their successes.

Since the first iteration of this book in 2017, a relatively new aspect of trauma research called *epigenetic trauma* has edged its way into the mainstream. This is a game-changer when working with the ancestral shadow, so let's look at it in detail.

Epigenetic Trauma

We now have scientific proof of what shamans and *sangomas* have been telling us for millennia: the traumas and fears of our ancestors can be passed down to us.

In a landmark 2013 study[2] published in the esteemed academic journal *Nature*, the reality of trauma being biologically passed down from parent to child was laid out in black and white.

The study used mice families to explore how traumatic experiences could become epigenetically encoded and passed down the generations.

Laboratory mice were trained to fear the scent of cherry blossom by being given electric shocks whenever the scent was released. They eventually came to associate the scent with pain, shuddering and reacting fearfully to the smell even without the electric shocks being given.

So far, so Pavlovian, but then something quite remarkable happened. When the traumatized mice reproduced, their offspring also reacted fearfully when they smelled cherry blossom, even though they had had no previous exposure to the scent. In fact, the baby mice had been separated from their parents at birth to rule out any learned behaviour that could explain the phenomenon.

The cherry blossom trauma response had been passed down to the next generation despite them never having had any negative association with the scent.

But it didn't stop there. When those second-generation mice had their own offspring, they also expressed fear when they smelled cherry blossom, even though they too had never had any contact with the scent, or with the grandparents who had initially been traumatized by it. The third generation of mice were reacting fearfully to a stimulus which they had no reason to fear.

When the team dissected the mice's brains they found there was a greater number of the neurons that detect cherry blossom scent, compared with control mice. This means that these mice were born into the world *neurologically predisposed* to be hypervigilant and fearful of the thing that had traumatized their ancestors.

So, is all lost? Are we simply destined to carry the trauma of our forefathers and then pass it down to our own children? Absolutely not. Although the cherry blossom study is well known, what is not so well known is the study that followed it.

In this later study,[3] the same scientists explored what would happen if the traumatized mice were helped to integrate their fear response by being repeatedly exposed to the cherry blossom scent but not being electrocuted.

Not only were the mice able to free themselves of their fear response and create new associations to the scent that were not traumatic, but this integration occurred at a genetic level: their offspring weren't afraid of the scent either.

When researchers looked at their sperm, they had lost their characteristic 'fearful' epigenetic signature after the desensitization process. And so, naturally, the pups of these mice also no longer showed the heightened sensitivity to the scent.

The ancestral trauma of the mice family line had been healed through exposure therapy, a kind of shadow work – scientific proof that we do not have to pass down ancestral trauma if we can find a way to integrate it ourselves.

My Grandmother's Footsteps

I looked out over the cliffs and thought how she would have seen the same sea. Same but different – separated by five generations. I was on the trail of my maternal ancestors, trying to uncover both the dark and golden shadow traits of my familial line as a way of further befriending and integrating my shadow.

I had arrived at the clifftop house on the Isle of Wight, off the south coast of the UK, where my great-great grandmother had once lived, and I was about to begin the three-mile journey to the tiny 11th-century church where her daughter had played the organ every Sunday. As I walked along the cliffs, I could feel an almost palpable energy that I thought might be from my ancestors.

Then, as if to confirm this hunch, I encountered a series of such strange signs and synchronicities within such a small space of time that I struggled to believe them. They included a street with the same name as my grandmother's street in London (although 100 miles apart), a six-inch Buddha statue embedded into a drystone wall (I still have no idea how to explain that) and finally a Spitfire fighter plane from the same era as my grandfather's time in the army, which flew overhead exactly as I arrived at the church (just in case I hadn't got the message yet).

I was sure of it now – my ancestors knew that I was calling to them and they were calling back to me, using perhaps the only means that ancestors can use: synchronicity, signs and Spitfire fighter planes.

I continued my research with photo albums, interviews with family members and even a DNA test to trace my genealogy. As I reviewed my ancestral line and reflected on my ancestors' lives, I saw shadow patterns emerging over and again: fierce female independence, strong fraternal bonds, bright creative flair for the golden and a whole load of secrets, lies and denial for the dark.

When I traced my family line, I found actors and performers on both sides of my ancestry: a vaudeville music troupe on my mum's and a circus troupe who performed for the Tsar of Russia on my dad's. No wonder I feel so at home on stage!

Just the process of becoming aware of and witnessing my ancestral shadow traits has changed me. Now, whenever I catch myself about to play out a familial shadow trait such as secrecy or denial, I pause and remind myself that I have a choice: to continue repeating this pattern or break it for the sake of my future family. This simple change has had profound effects.

So, let's explore how to begin integrating our ancestral shadow, step by step.

Exercise: Exploring the Ancestral Shadow

This exercise takes a bit of planning, but it's one that I strongly encourage you to do. Take it slowly and playfully. I advise exploring the happier aspects of your family history first as a way of building a solid foundation of gratitude. This will help support the weight of any heavier aspects that you may uncover.

If you know that there is trauma or abuse in your family's past, feel free to simply acknowledge this when you encounter it, rather than delve deeply into it. As always, feel free to share your experience with a therapist, coach or trusted friend.

Step 1

Ideally, arrange to spend an afternoon (or more if you like) with an older family member or close friend of the family who has a good knowledge of your ancestral history.

Spend your time together journeying back into your family's past using photo albums, artefacts or simply remembered stories to help you to understand who your ancestors were.

You needn't travel back very far if it's not possible. Even just tracing your line back as far as your great-grandmother can be more than enough. This exercise is really about intention, and the healing will occur at an energetic level.

Step 2

If you can, make a pilgrimage back to the land of your ancestors. You may have ancestors from many different places, so just choose one place, perhaps the one that you know most about or the one that's easiest for you to get to. You are much more likely to do this exercise if you travel to an accessible place rather than halfway across the globe, but either is fine, of course.

Walk in the footsteps of your ancestors and visit their birthplaces and/or grave sites. Act like an explorer, seeing, with friendly curiosity, how far back into the past you can go as you walk on the same earth that they once walked upon. Ask local people if they knew your family or remember your family name, go into the local records office and see if you can find your ancestors' births on the registers. Be creative; the aim is to uncover their story and to pay homage to their memory.

Step 3

While you are making this pilgrimage, take some time to reflect on both the dark and the golden shadows of your family lines.

Ask yourself the following questions, based on the information you have gathered and any insights you have had:

- 'Are there any recurring dark shadow patterns or themes that I can find in my family line?' (Adultery, criminality, shame, lies, trauma or deceit?)

- 'Are there any recurring golden shadow patterns or themes that I can find in my family line?' (Talents, remarkable traits, spiritual connections, creativity or charity?)

- 'Can I recognize any of these dark or golden aspects in myself or do I see any of them playing out in my current family relationships?' If so, then for now simply bear witness to them and send them your love.

- 'What insights does the story of my ancestors offer me in relation to my current family situation?'

- 'What golden traits of my ancestors am I ready to invoke and embody today?'
- 'What dark shadow traits of my ancestors am I ready to let go of today?'

Step 4

Now, write a letter to your ancestors in which you acknowledge their stories, send them your love and respectfully state your intention to release any and all ancestral patterns that no longer serve you.

Be sure to include an acknowledgement of any dark shadow themes that you noticed, while also acknowledging those that you also embody or have embodied, and write a statement of intent to let those traits go. Putting this down in writing is a powerful way of setting the intention to clear the ancestral line of dark shadow material.

Do the same with any golden themes that you noticed and make a declaration to your ancestors to invoke and embody more of those golden traits from now on.

Let your ancestors know of any insights that their story has led to about your current family and, most importantly, be sure to thank them. Thank them not only for any great deeds they committed or golden potential that they embodied, but also just for surviving, for staying alive, for if any one of them had died early, you would literally not exist.

You might also like to draw a picture of your family line, starting with yourself and your parents and going back as far as you like. Draw a little stick-person for each family member and then write their name by them (see opposite). This is a way to honour your family line symbolically.

Find a way to 'post' this letter and picture by reading them out loud to your reflection in a mirror and then ceremonially burning them, before dedicating the beneficial energy of the practice to your past and future ancestors.

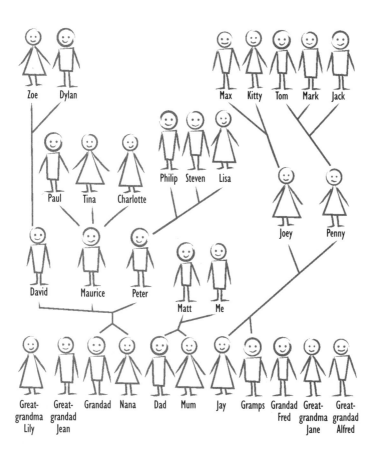

My ancestral line

Wherever we have gathered our shadow material from, whether it is ancestral or self-created, we have to take responsibility for who we are. As I've said before, who we are is not our fault, but it is our responsibility, and our ability to respond to our current situation relies upon us making friends with the lineage that we've come from. We are the only ones who can integrate our ancestral shadow and, more importantly, the only ones who can prevent the recurring familial shadow patterns from being passed down the line. The future is in our hands.

RECAPS AND REFLECTIONS

✓ The traumatic experiences of our ancestors can be passed down to us through our genes.

✓ Integrating our own traumas before we have children will prevent the legacy of trauma being passed on.

✓ Healing our ancestral shadow frees us from the ghosts in our DNA.

✓ Paying homage to our ancestors helps to activate the golden potentials they passed down to us.

» Are you able to set a date to explore your ancestral shadow?

» Can you think of any aspects of epigenetic trauma that you may have inherited from your family line?

» What golden traits might you have inherited from your ancestors?

CHAPTER 14

EXPLORING THE SEXUAL SHADOW

'Everything in the world is about sex,
except sex. Sex is about power.'

OSCAR WILDE (ATTRIB.)

Nowadays, at an outer level we see sex and sexualized images every time we look at our social media feed or switch on the TV, and yet at an inner level there is an underlying and almost universally experienced suppression of our sexuality. Suppression creates shadow, and when this is combined with the fear, shame and even trauma that are so often tied up in our personal relationship with sex, it comes as no surprise that our shadow will almost always have sexual content.

Was there anything to do with sex on the inside of your mask? Was there anything to do with sex in your bag that you drag? Have you ever suppressed your sexual urges or been shamed sexually? Most of us will answer 'yes' to one or all of those questions, and that's why most of us will benefit from exploring our sexual shadow.

For many of us, sexual experiences and the projection of sexual dogmas onto us by early-life authority figures will have created some of our densest shadow content. When we add to that the heavy shadows of sexual shame, unfulfilled sexual desire and the gold of our true sexual identity that many non-heteronormative people may have had to hide in their shadow for decades, it seems that looking at our relationship to sex is obligatory if we want to integrate our shadow.

Sexual energy is one of the most potent creative forces in existence and in fact none of us would exist without it. So how can we harness that energy and unlock its creative power? Through masks, mirrors and an ancient shamanic practice.

Masks in the Mirror

Apart from Tibetan Buddhism, the spiritual lineage I've had the most personal experience of is the ancient shamanic Toltec Mexihca tradition of Mexico. I have co-facilitated many workshops on shadow work, lucid dreaming and conscious dying with my friend Sergio Magaña, who is a shamanic teacher based in Mexico City. Sergio is the author of several books, including *The Toltec Secret*, and in 2013 he was named as the UNESCO representative for the preservation of the Toltec Mexihca tradition. Definitely check him out if you're interested in Mexican shamanism.

In the Toltec tradition, as in Tibetan Buddhism and Jungian psychology, it is believed that in order to integrate the shadow we first need to accept that we have these aspects within us and then be prepared to face them through practices that ask us to look directly into our shadow side.

Some of the shamanic practices that I've learned from Sergio are pretty far-out, including ingesting the powdered body of a rattlesnake in order to invite the spirit of the serpent into dreams and ritual dances under full moons to align the subtle energy centres. One of the most powerful (and totally far-out) practices that I've been taught by him involves wearing masks, talking into a mirror and downloading your entire sexual story as a way of transforming your sexual shadow and regaining your sexual power.

'Wait, we do what exactly?'

The set-up of this exercise can seem rather bizarre, but stay with me, because once you see how it works, it will all make sense. We're now in the transformation part of this book, so we are going to go pretty deep, but we'll emerge transformed.

Essentially, to do this practice you stand or sit in front of a mirror, wearing a series of masks, and talk out loud for 36 minutes about your relationship to sex and sexuality. You do this every day for at least nine days straight.

The aim is to download the entire story of your sexual history and all the shadow content that it contains from the darkness of your unconscious into the light of your awareness. Why? To help you to dis-identify with your sexual story, which will allow you to be free of the shame, trauma and fear that it may contain and create space for the power, joy and freedom of your true sexual energy to shine.

'Sounds great, but what's up with the masks?

The idea behind wearing the masks is that your sense of self-identification is strongly linked to your face. Think about it. When you imagine a person, it's their face that you see in your mind's eye, isn't it? Not their elbow or their feet.

Your face is synonymous with your ego-identity, and so by covering it with a mask while you recount your sexual story to the mirror, you see and hear it being recounted not by *you* but by another face, and so your story and your ego-identity start to become separated. At a subliminal level, your mind starts to dis-identify with the story being told and with all the co-authors of that story – the partners, lovers, parents and friends who added to the narrative. This dis-identification releases the stranglehold that your past sexual experiences can still have on you and can dissolve habits, traumas and energetic blocks pertaining to your sexual history in a very powerful way.

I know this exercise sounds crazy when you first read about it, but it does actually make sense. It's basically about talking through all your past sexual experiences as a way of releasing the underlying energy. It allows them to be witnessed and processed, and any shame to be released, because, as we know, shame gains its power from being unspeakable.

The crux of the technique really comes from wearing the masks, though. They are essential, because they break the link between your face, the symbol of your identity, and the sexual story being told.

In fact, if you did this exercise *without* wearing a mask, then you would simply further concretize the connection between you and your sexual story.

When I asked Sergio what we should speak about apart from our sexual history, he said, 'Talk about the social, religious and scientific paradigms that you have been exposed to and how they've affected your sexuality. The mask will help you to stop identifying with your sexual story and be free of this conditioning. Talk about everything you have ever been told about sex. Talk about your positive sexual experiences and your sexual fantasies too. You will release your trapped sexual energy, the most powerful energy you have, and harness it for your shadow work and spiritual practice.'[1]

My Journey into the Mirror

If you're still having reservations about this exercise, let me share my story with you, because I had reservations too!

As a sceptical Buddhist, and a sceptical British Buddhist at that, this whole mask/mirror/sex thing just seemed a bit too 'woo-woo' for me. I just couldn't imagine how talking about my sexual history in front of a mirror while wearing a mask could have any psychological benefit at all.

Eventually I gave it a shot, though. For the first five minutes of the first session I really thought I was wasting my time and I felt genuinely embarrassed to be offloading my sexual baggage in front of a bathroom mirror while wearing an ill-fitting *Lion King* mask.

But soon interesting things started to happen. My reflection started to morph and the image of the mask became almost animated. Then, as I spoke, my sexual story actually began to sound like someone else's. It was strange, but it was almost as if I was hearing my voice talking about a stranger's sexual problems. I could feel myself starting to dis-identify with the story. So much of it had happened so long ago. Why was I still judging myself for stuff I'd done as a teenager? How could I blame my 10-year-old self for not knowing how to kiss properly?

Soon I found myself talking about sexual shame that I hadn't recalled in over 20 years, and by the seventh day of the practice I was having quite profound insights into my relationship with sexuality.

I saw how my sexual story had started early on in life. I remembered the first time I'd seen porn and how I'd felt scared by it, the time I'd felt sexually attracted to another boy, the long conversations with my mum about how menstruation worked and the little girl I'd fallen in love with at the video-games arcade when I was eight years old.

So many memories had been buried, unconsciously weighing me down, shackling me to a myth of who I thought I was.

I felt so much lighter afterwards, more authentic and more aware of how my sexual story had been shaped by circumstance, shame and a longing for love.

Lovability/sex-ability

One of the deepest insights I had while doing this exercise came through tracing a long-standing sexual complex – the belief that I had to be 'good' in bed in order to be lovable – back to my first kiss at the age of 10. My friend and I were playing 'spin the bottle' with a group of older girls, and as I was experiencing my first kiss, everybody was laughing at me as I struggled to work out the dynamics of kissing and ended up making embarrassing slurping noises.

I hadn't spoken of that incident for years. And yet I realized that afterwards 10-year-old Charlie had made some sort of unconscious pledge to be 'good' at sexual stuff so that the pain of that humiliation never happened again. In so doing, I had created a deep shadow complex around sexuality and self-worth.

Suddenly all the irrationally amplified feelings of anger, despair and unlovability that I had felt in dozens of sexual relationships over the past 30 years whenever I had felt that my sexual performance had been less than 'good' made sense. The reason that I would act like an angry confused child in those moments was that once that trauma was triggered, I was 10 years old again, back in that 'spin the bottle' circle, feeling humiliated.

Simply tracing the origin of this complex, naming it 'lovability/ sex-ability' and then witnessing it with compassionate acceptance released the stranglehold that it had over me. Remembering that single buried memory changed my life.

This 'original wound' of shame then led me to start talking to the mirror about porn and the addictive relationship that I had had with it during my twenties. Research tells us that 'sexual rejection is the hallmark of masculine shame'[2] and one psychotherapist has even suggested that the reason why men are drawn to porn is because 'you feel like you're getting what you need and crucially there is no risk of rejection'.[3] For me, that was very true: porn was a safe sexual experience free from the devastating possibility of being rejected.

Owning our sexual story can be hard, but not nearly as hard as trying to keep it hidden. So I strongly encourage everyone to do this exercise, not just those who know that they have lots of sexual shadow material, but also those who don't, because we often have no idea how much dark and golden sexual shadow material we have until we do this exercise. In fact, it is often workshop participants who have seemed the most buttoned up and emotionally suppressed who have gained the most from doing it.

Exercise: Sexual Shadow Masks
. . . .

The original version of this practice is called 'The Venerable Old Man' and requires that you do the entire practice in one marathon session of 12 hours straight! (*For a full description of it, see Sergio Magaña*, The Toltec Secret.[4])

We're not going to do that version, though, we're going to do a specially adapted one which Sergio has approved in which we spend 36 minutes in front of the mirror for at least nine days straight or a maximum of 21 days straight.

You might be thinking, *Why 36 minutes?* In the ancient Mexihca tradition each 24-hour cycle is broken up into 11 fractions of the day and nine of the night. This led to nine becoming the number of the night, darkness and the shadow. This number is then multiplied by four, a number significant because of the four moon phases and the four seasons, to get the special number 36!

Step 1

Get yourself at least three different masks. They can be any type you like, but make sure that they fully cover your face. Cheap masks from a toy shop will be fine, but if you want to use fancier ones, then go for it. When I did it, I chose particularly ridiculous farm animal ones to help bring humour to the process and to make sure that I definitely did not look like myself.

Step 2

Set an alarm for 36 minutes later, put on one of the masks first and then stand or sit in front of a mirror.

Look into the mirror and talk, out loud and in the first person, about all there is to know about your relationship to sex and sexuality.

Talk about absolutely everything: turn-ons, taboos, perversions, sexual orientation and your entire sexual history from every angle you can imagine. Talk about everything you know, everything you have been taught, been programmed to believe and truly believe about sex and sexuality.

Explore your fears and fantasies. Be totally uncensored – nothing is off-limits. Say the unsayable and offer any and all sexual shame to the mirror. Remember that shame derives its power from being unspeakable, and when we speak about it, we lessen the power it has over us.

Essentially, whatever you would say to a sexologist or psychotherapist is what you can say to the reflection in the mirror.

You can do this 36-minute session at any time of day or night, but doing it before bed allows you to weave the thread of integration directly into your dreams too.

Step 3

Repeat Step 2 for at least nine days straight. You can do it at different times each day, but make sure that you do one session per 24 hours for at least nine days straight.

Change masks whenever you like, but be sure not to do it while looking in the mirror, for the illusion may be broken.

If you feel you need more than nine days, then keep going for 36 minutes every day until you feel that there is nothing more to be said, up to a maximum of 21 days.

Here are some tips for this exercise:

- If you like, choose specific aspects of your sexuality and spend a whole 36-minute session on each one; for example, do one session on sexual fantasies, one on masturbation, one on your worst sexual experiences and one on what you were taught about sexuality as a child. Or you can just be spontaneous and see what comes up.

- The more you say, the more you hear; the more you hear, the more you transform.

- Tears and laughter are part of the process, so be prepared to go deep but also keep it playful.

- Allow yourself to really experience the emotional energy of past events, because *feeling the feeling leads to healing.*

- Be creative. Thirty-six minutes can seem like quite a long time to be talking uninterrupted, so periods of silence, just watching the reflection, are fine too.

- If trauma or abuse are part of your sexual history, go gently and feel free simply to acknowledge the abuse rather than going deeply into the memory. If any distressing memories surface that you feel require professional help, don't hesitate to seek a therapist or trained professional.

- Keep going. On some days it will seem as though nothing is happening and then the next day you'll have a breakthrough.

- This is a shamanic practice that dates back over 1,000 years. So, take solace in the knowledge that you're connecting to the power of an ancient lineage.

Step 4

Although not found in the Toltec tradition, an additional step that I found particularly beneficial was, when the mask and mirror work was finished, creating a simple stick-person drawing of my sexual history (a bit like a family tree of sexual partners) and then ceremonially burning it while stating:

> *'I release any and all non-beneficial energetic ties to every person pictured here.'*

And finally, be extra-attentive to your dreams while you are doing this practice, because you may find, especially if you do the exercise before bed, that your dreams are affected by whatever you have been telling the mirror.

This is because when you release and dis-identify with your emotional patterns, your dreams, which are dictated by these patterns to a large degree, will naturally start to change. As you download the memories that you recount to the mirror, you free up space in your unconscious mind, allowing lucid dreaming and dreams of insight to manifest more readily.

• •

Real-Life Feedback

A navy officer called Gareth found this exercise to be particularly powerful. After his first few nights, he emailed me, saying:

> *'Woah... that was hardcore! The first chunk was difficult to look at: father, mother, sexual role-models, porn, gender, self-esteem... I saw my dreams respond too. That night I got*

a clear message from the dream state. It said: "Build your temple because now you are ready to fill your temple."'

A woman from South Africa who had experienced sexual abuse emailed me to say:

'I did the sexual shadow mask exercise exactly as you instructed, but it was very, very difficult.

For the first time in my life I said out loud (in whispered sobs) every single one of the terrible things I had experienced. I realized quickly that without the masks I could not have done so... they made me feel safer?

I don't know why is was so powerful... It was such a surreal experience... something about the amount of time, the masks, the number of days... and saying it all out loud... Something massive shifted.

I can't say that I was cured of my depression and anxiety instantly, but it led to me reaching out for the first time in my life and seeking the help of a qualified psychologist.

Now, five years later, my life is transformed. I am very happy. Thank you.'

Calling the Shadow into Our Dreams

In life, most of us don't want to face the shadow, so we deny it. In dreams, it can't be denied, because it's on its home turf. Knowing that we can't consciously avoid it, as we do when awake, it moves towards us, wanting to be known.

The appearance of the shadow in our dreams should be seen as a great opportunity, offering us the chance to embrace our shadow aspects as part of ourselves and to encounter them fearlessly.

So far we have learned how to recall our dreams, diarize our dreams and decode our shadow in our dreams. Now that we have a solid foundation, let's move on to something a bit more transformational: calling the shadow into our dreams.

You might imagine that doing so would be like asking for a nightmare, but remember, our shadow is made up of both our golden and our dark aspects.

A few years back I called the shadow into my dreams, using the technique opposite, and what appeared was a perfect example of how something can be pure gold to some and pure darkness to others: I dreamed of meeting Donald Trump. He came over to me and asked me who I was voting for, and when I explained that I was British and couldn't vote in the US election, he was jovial and warm-hearted towards me. As he shook my hand, I remember feeling almost annoyed by how friendly and nice he seemed. He wasn't how I had expected him to be at all.

Trump is a very interesting dream character to decode, because he's so divisive. For many people he will represent their golden shadow – individuality, being great again, doing things differently – whereas to others he will be a dark shadow representation of their unseen racism, misogyny and trauma.

So, your shadow won't always manifest in your dreams in a clear-cut way, but however it appears, it needs your love, not your vitriol. Perhaps the same could be said of Donald Trump?

Exercise: Calling the Shadow into Your Dreams

Lie down in bed, ready for sleep, and close your eyes. The aim of this practice is to stay in the hypnagogic state mindfully without entering into the sleep that lies beyond it.

As you rest in the hypnagogic state, recite over and over in your mind:

'Shadow, come to me, I am ready to meet you!'

or:

'Shadow, show yourself – enter my dreams!'

After a few minutes of recitation, allow yourself to fall asleep, saturated with the energy and intention of your affirmation.

The next morning, or whenever you wake, write your dreams down and then go through the process of decoding them to see how your shadow appeared (*see p.111*).

KEY POINTS AND REFLECTIONS

✓ Sexual energy is one of the most potent creative forces in existence.

✓ Owning our sexual story can be hard, but not nearly as hard as trying to keep it hidden.

✓ Both dark sexual shame and unexpressed sexual gold form a big part of many people's shadows.

✓ Even 1,000 years ago, shamans knew that we had to be proactive to integrate our sexual shadow.

» Do you feel ready to explore your sexual shadow?

» How many days do you think you will need to do this practice – just nine or more?

» Can you commit to buying yourself three masks today? This is often the step that people have most unconscious resistance to.

» How might your life be different if you were able to integrate your sexual shadow?

CHAPTER 15

DEATH: THE ULTIMATE SHADOW

'Everybody should do two things in their lifetime: to observe death and to consider what it will be like to die.'

ALAN WATTS[1]

Each day 150,000 people do it and one day you will do it too, but when was the last time you reflected on the fact that you will die?

For many people, fear of death is the ultimate shadow.

In the West, most of us live for about 1,000 months or so. A thousand months, that's all, and then we die.

Death is the great equalizer, a shared commonality of human experience. We will all die. Definitely and successfully. And yet we hardly ever talk about it. Why is that? Fear, mostly. But also denial, suppression, trauma and shame, which are of course the building blocks of the shadow. Death anxiety, as it's called, is for many people one of their greatest shadows, and so transforming it can bring the greatest benefits.

The concept of death anxiety was popularized in the West by Ernest Becker in his 1973 book *The Denial of Death*. It manifests most obviously as just not wanting to talk about or think about death, but it can also be expressed more subtly through a fear of the death of relationships, a fear of the death of our identity as we grow older, or even a fear of stepping into our golden potential due to the death of who we thought we were.

We will all have to face death – we have no choice in that – but what we *can* choose is how to face it. If we are able truly to transform our fear of death, we will transform one of the densest shadows we hold.

So, I invite you to think about death. This isn't intended to make you feel sad, it's intended to help you overcome your sadness. The death of others is of course saddening, and remembering loved ones who have passed away can be extremely painful, but I'm talking about contemplating your *own* death here, rather than other people's.

If you can bring the fear, shame, suppression and denial of death out of the shadows and into conscious awareness, you will release and reclaim huge amounts of energy. And, if you can transform your fear of death, a new perspective on life opens up to you.

THE SCIENCE OF MORTALITY AWARENESS

Research published in the *Journal of Applied Psychology and Social Science* in 2007 showed that 'death anxiety' led people to be 'more racist, nationalistic, homophobic and more likely to support violence against others'.[2] It explained: 'Self-esteem is the primary buffer which serves to protect humans from fear of their own mortality and when faced with reminders of mortality, human beings will favour and draw closer to their own kind.'[3] This often results in increased levels of racism and tribalism.

Luckily for us, though, becoming more aware of our own mortality integrates this death anxiety and directly counteracts these harmful 'death-denying' symptoms.

A more recent study, conducted in 2016 by researchers at the University of Arizona in the United States, found that athletes who completed a questionnaire about death and facing up to their own mortality showed a '40 per cent improvement in their subsequent personal performance'.[4]

Another experiment in the same study asked basketball players to take part in a one-minute basket-shooting challenge. Half of the subjects received a subtle but conscious reminder of death: the researcher was wearing a T-shirt with a white skull on it, along with other visual signifiers of mortality. Fascinatingly, 'those who'd seen the "death" T-shirt performed approximately 30 per cent better than those who hadn't'.[5]

Scientific proof that facing our fear of death by thinking about our own mortality makes us live more fully and effectively.

My Journey into Death

I have been fascinated by death ever since a near-death experience caused by a drugs overdose that I had when I was a teenager.

I had the classic 'life flashing before my eyes' experience before entering an infinite void wherein I was asked, 'Charlie, do you want to live or do you want to die?'

It was, without doubt, the most intense and horrifying and life-changing event of my life and it kickstarted me on the path of spirituality and towards a fascination with death.

After studying and practising Buddhism since my teens, I ended up living in a Buddhist centre, Kagyu Samye Dzong London, for seven years and joining a team of volunteers there called The Bardo Group, who offer practical assistance to those approaching the end of life. We help to organize the spiritual care, funerals and after-death prayers of people in and around London who ask for our support.[6]

I've since trained as a Buddhist chaplain (yup, Charlie the Chaplain), helped to lead many funerals and had the privilege to be by the side of several people as they took their last breath. Being with someone as they die is one of the greatest privileges there is, and one of the best ways to integrate the shadowy fear of death.

The reason death is scary is that we are not familiar with it. A hundred years ago most people would have seen dozens of dead bodies by the time they were teenagers, as open-casket funerals were common and most people died at home. But nowadays we push death into the shadows, meaning that there are many grown adults who have never seen a dead body.

With familiarity comes fearlessness, and so the best gift we can give someone who is dying is often not just sympathy, but also familiarity. Becoming familiar with death and dead bodies will not only lessen our own fear, but also prevent us from projecting that fear onto the dying people we will inevitably come into contact with.

If you are really serious about integrating your shadow, then death must be faced and embraced. So I urge you to consider doing all you can to habituate yourself to it, perhaps volunteering at a hospice or offering your time to a palliative care charity or checking out the brilliant Death Café movement, which invites you to talk about death over tea and cake.[7] Every year at Kagyu Samye Dzong London we run an 'Embracing Death and Dying' day, a full day of talks, workshops and art exhibitions on the theme of death. Consider this your invitation to the next one.

If these suggestions are too much, then at least try to read about death, talk about death, celebrate death and definitely do the practical meditations around death that we explore on the following pages.

Drowning Dogs

During the 1890s, the Russian physiologist Ivan Pavlov was investigating salivation in dogs in response to being fed. In his famous study, whenever he gave food to his dogs, he also rang a bell so that the dogs came to associate the bell with food. After a while, he rang the bell on its own and, as you might expect, the dogs salivated, as they unconsciously associated the bell with food. Pavlov had programmed a new habitual pattern into their minds, sometimes called a 'conditioned reflex'. It's from this well-known experiment that we get the phrase 'Pavlovian response'.

What is less well known is that during the experiments Pavlov's laboratories in Leningrad were flooded by rising river levels. Pavlov's assistants came to the panicking dogs' rescue and although some dogs died, some of them were saved.

Then a very unexpected thing happened. Their traumatic brush with death left the surviving dogs changed. They no longer salivated when the bell was rung: their conditioned reflexes had disappeared. Their minds had been freed from their conditioning by the shock of facing their own mortality.

Hostage survivors, death-row inmates and those who have had near-death experiences often display a similar phenomenon. By facing our own death, we can shift some of our own conditioning.

We can get a taste of this deconditioning process simply by *imagining* that our death is coming soon, which is exactly what I invite you to do in the next exercise.

One Week Left

'Of all the mindfulness meditations,
that on death is supreme.'
Buddha, in the Mahaparanirvana Sutra

If you knew that you were going to die in one week from now, how would you spend your last seven days?

Considering this question is one of the most powerful shadow integration exercises there is. Meditating on death and dying can help us to stop wasting our time on meaningless activities and start living our lives more fully. It draws into focus the unfulfilled golden shadow that we have yet to embody while also integrating the dark shadow fear of death.

We have to plan for the future, of course, but if we can at least imagine that we have limited time, then we might find that our life becomes much more alive.

We might start by showing people that we love them. Although we may have visions of loved ones gathered round our deathbed, listening intently as we say what needs to be said, palliative care expert Dr Angela Halley told me that:

'In the last few hours many people can't even talk, let alone engage in the complex thought processes of reconciling relationships.

That's why it's so important to do all the regrets and reconciliation stuff before we start dying. For most people, "I forgive you", "I'm sorry", "Thank you" and "I love you" are the four things that need to be said, so don't wait, say them now while you're healthy.[8]

Exercise: Seven Days Left to Live
. . . .

You can find this exercise set to music and guided by my voice on my website (www.charliemorley.com/shadowexercises) under the title 'Seven Days Left to Live,' but feel free to guide yourself using the steps below too.

Step 1

Allow yourself to relax deeply.

Focus on your breathing and count at least three deep but relaxed breaths.

Step 2

If you knew that you were going to die in seven days from now, what would you do? Take some time simply to rest with the question in your mind.

Who would you call? Where would you go? To whom would you apologize? What would you change in your life so that you could die at peace with the world? What niggly little conflict would you try to resolve? What wrong would you put right? What fear would you face? Be realistic, but be optimistic. If you knew that you were going to die in seven days, how would you spend your last week?

Step 3

Now focus in on three or more specific things that you would do, say or make happen if you had one week left to live. They don't have to be big things, just personal to you. Decide on three or more things and take some time to note them down, if you like.

Step 4

Finally, if there is one thing on your list that you can *realistically*, *safely* and *beneficially* do within the next seven days of your life, will you do it? Why wait?

If so, then I encourage you to do it. Don't wait until you are on your deathbed – make it happen now, within the next week of your life.

Step 5

As always, if it feels right to do so, dedicate your practice to the benefit of all beings, using the statement:

> *'I dedicate the beneficial energy generated by this exercise to the benefit of all beings.'*

••••••••••••••••••••••••••••••••••••••

By waking up to death, we start to wake up to life. We become aware of the limitations of time. We realize that we don't have long to make our mark, to offer something of value to the human story. So don't wait till you actually have one week left to live, say what needs to be said *now*, do what needs to be done *now*, start living the life you want to live *now*. Why wait?

Real-Life Feedback

Robert, a German poet and lucid dreaming facilitator, told me how doing this exercise led to an 'Aha!' moment as he realized that he had never really said goodbye to his deceased father and that this was what he needed to do if he had seven days left to live.

He said:

> 'At his grave at the funeral, I clearly remember that I intentionally said, "Thank you", but I never really said goodbye. I was avoiding saying my farewell and letting him go. Suddenly, while doing the Seven Days Left exercise, it was so clear in front of me, this felt like a missing puzzle piece. I needed to say goodbye.'

The Life Review

> 'Let us not wait to review our lives on our deathbed.
> Let us finish our business before our lease is up.'
> STEPHEN LEVINE[9]

The shadow is not fixed. We're constantly either adding to it or integrating it, so if we really want to transform it at a deep level, we need to look at our lives as a whole.

In this exercise you will be asked to review your life. Yup, the whole thing.

Basically, you're going to take a massive piece of paper and create a huge spider diagram of your entire life from birth till now, documenting every significant memory that you can recall from every five-year chapter of your life, so that by the end every major event of your life is laid out before you.

The aim of this life review is to bear witness to what changed you, what broke you, what helped you, who loved you and what you made of it all. Write down not just what happened, but how you felt about what happened. By doing this, you witness and 'download' your past in a structured, compassionate way, and as the memories arise, you need do nothing more than bear witness to them with love and acceptance for their energy to be integrated.

Reviewing your entire life from birth to the present moment and taking stock of it all is a brilliant way to transform past shadows, become aware of recurring patterns and make friends with the past.

With so much shadow material stored in forgotten memory and unconscious habits, the life review will also allow you to spot shadow traits and emotional patterns that have recurred *unconsciously* throughout your life.

Consciously bearing witness to your past helps liberate regret and shame from the dark shadow while highlighting the powerful potentials that lie in the golden one. You remember your forgotten mistakes with forgiveness and our forgotten light with joy.

It's also a brilliant way to transform the shadow of death anxiety. How? Because when you do a full life review, you are creating a slowed-down version of the 'life flashing before your eyes' phenomenon found in many near-death experiences. This allows you to embody the huge shifts in perspective and insights about your life that many near-death experiencers report (but without the nearly dying bit!)

The First 32 Years

I first did the life review when I was 32 years old, during a three-month meditation retreat. Each day for a week I would spend an hour or so documenting each five-year chapter of my life, listing every major life event, significant memory, noteworthy moment, emotional trauma and forgotten joy that I could remember.

As I reviewed my life, I remembered lost loves, forgotten friends and seemingly insignificant events that had created huge opportunities. I was amazed at how much I'd simply forgotten.

But I was also shocked and ashamed by some of the stuff I'd done – the horrible things I'd said to people, the harsh way I'd treated others, the soft hearts I'd trampled on and the kindnesses that I'd never appreciated. It was painful at times and I cried a lot.

As I did this, I trusted in what Stephen Levine says in his brilliant book *One Year to Live* – that if we allow ourselves to really feel the pain of those we hurt, while sending them our love and compassion, both parties receive healing.

By the time I got to reviewing my mid-twenties, my dark shadow patterns suddenly became so obvious: I had a recurring theme around fear of abandonment, another around infidelity and another around feeling constantly guilty and then projecting that guilt onto others.

My golden shadow patterns revealed themselves too: I could see that I was happiest when I was not only creating, but helping others through what I had created.

I thought I knew what kind of a life I had had, but it wasn't until I put it all down in front of me in a huge interconnected spider diagram that I really saw my life as it was: so much grief and pain, but also so much good fortune and happiness.

As I went on reviewing each five-year chapter, I made friends with my blame and my shame, and I gave thanks to those who had helped me. When I'd finished and I looked back over my first 32 years, I saw beyond doubt two truths: i) meeting life with love makes it easier; and ii) everyone is always just trying their best.

This final exercise of the book is quite a biggie, but it's well worth doing.

It's only when we see our whole life laid out before us that we can fully recognize our recurring shadow patterns and trace them back to their source. By doing this, we are able to witness those patterns and change those behaviours going forward.

Taking stock of our life up till now is the perfect way of taking the reins back of a life that may often seem out of our control. The life review allows us to see how much of our life has been left unlived and, crucially, gives us the chance to change that from now on. It allows us to start living every day not as if it's our last, but as if it's our first, with the eyes of a child, seeing everything for the first time.

Exercise: The Life Review

This exercise requires that you document as much of your life as you can onto a big piece of paper (A1 or poster size works well), or digitally if you prefer. You can use words, images, diagrams and even collage to create this review. Be creative – you can't get it wrong.

It can either be done all in one day or spread over several days, but before you begin, here are my top tips on the process:

- *Feel into the memory.* Don't just explore what happened, but also how you *felt* about what happened.

- *Use photos.* Photo albums can be used to help spark your memories.

- *Be a loving witness.* Try to look back over your life without judgement or blame.

- *Don't grasp too hard.* What you can't remember is often as telling as what you can. There's no need to strive to find memories; just allow as many as want to reveal themselves to do so.

- *Mine for gold.* Be sure to recall the successes, achievements, loves and inspirations of each chapter. But also be aware of your unlived life: in what areas of life have you limited the full expression of your gold?

- *Look to your dreams.* A practice that recapitulates so many forgotten and unconscious memories is bound to have an effect on your dreams, so be sure to stay open and attentive to them on the nights that follow this exercise.

- *Allow it all.* Aspire to house all your memories under a roof of love held up by the three pillars of acceptance, friendliness and kindness, but when anger or regret arise, as they naturally will, give them equal space to display themselves.

- *There's no need to lift the lid.* If you know that there is trauma or abuse in your past, feel free simply to acknowledge those memories if and when you encounter them, without feeling any pressure to lift the lid on them intentionally. And as always, be sure to seek the support of a qualified therapist or trusted friend if and when needed.

Step 1

Spend time documenting every memorable event from your birth to the present day in five-year chapters – every significant moment, noteworthy event, joy, challenge, friendship, upset and achievement.

You can do this as a long list or as a spider diagram or mind map. Use words or pictures and work on paper or digitally, either is fine.

You don't have to work chronologically. Memories from one five-year chapter may arise while you are working on another, so feel free to skip between chapters.

Accept all memories, great or small. The fact that you remembered a particular event during this exercise is testament to its significance.

Take it slowly and playfully. I advise exploring the happier memories of each chapter first as a way of building a solid foundation of gratitude.

Spend anything from 20 minutes to several hours documenting each five-year chapter, but be sure to give yourself enough time to sit in forgetfulness too. Long-lost memories may take time to surface.

Step 2

At the end of each five-year chapter, review it and simply bear witness to it. The energy of the past is integrated through the act of friendly observation, so simply witness the memories without trying to change them

Whenever you come across a happy memory, take time to imagine the person that was central to it and send them your love and gratitude. Bring them into your awareness and say, either mentally or out loud:

'Thank you. May you be happy and well. I send you my love.'

Similarly, when you come across a painful memory, you may like to imagine the person or being that was central to it and, if you can, just bring them into your awareness and say, either mentally or out loud:

'I see you and I let you go. May you be
happy and well. I send you my love.'

Step 3

Next, for each five-year chapter, ask yourself:

- 'What are the dominant emotional themes of this period?'

- 'Are there any dark shadow traits being created or played out in this chapter?' If so note them down.

- 'Are there any golden shadow traits being created or played out in this chapter?' If so note them down.

Step 4

Once you have completed the life review right up to the present day, ask yourself the following questions and note down your answers:

- 'When were the times that I felt most alive? And what has that taught me about myself?'

- 'When in my life was I following my joy and living a life I loved? And when in my life was I living a life I didn't love?'

- 'What lessons have I learned from my life?' Pick five top lessons if you can.

- 'When have I felt most in my element and most authentic? And when I have I felt most lost, most inauthentic?'

- 'What things would I do differently if I could do them again, and can I make a commitment to embody that different way of doing things going forward?'

Dedication

If it feels right to do so, take a moment to dedicate all the goodness in your life to the benefit of all beings, using the statement:

> *'I dedicate the beneficial energy generated by*
> *this exercise to the benefit of all beings.'*

Once you have completed the life review, you can be proud to know that you have done what most people only get to do on their deathbed: you have reviewed your life story, and in doing so, you not only get to transform the shadows within it, but you also get to co-author the rest of it.

And finally, I want to leave you with one last idea: *kintsukuroi*. This is a Japanese term meaning 'golden repair' and refers to the art of repairing broken pottery with a kind of resin made with powdered gold. You can actually see this displayed on the cover of this book. When a pot cracks, rather than being seen as a fault, it is embraced as an opportunity to make it more beautiful and, with the addition of gold, literally more precious than before.

As you look back over your life story and see the cracks of regret or fractures of remembered heartache, take the opportunity to fill those cracks with the gold of love and compassion. This will make your story even more precious than before.

RECAPS AND REFLECTIONS

✓ You will only live for about 1,000 months. Don't waste a single moment more.

✓ Integrating your death anxiety will make you less prejudiced, kinder and better at stuff.

✓ A life review creates a kind of slowed-down version of the 'life flashing before your eyes' phenomenon found in many near-death experiences.

» If there is something on your 'seven days left' list that you can actually do in the next seven days, will you do it?

» Out of 10, what is your current level of death anxiety?

» Are you ready to do the life review?

CONCLUSION

'And where we had thought to find an
abomination we shall find a god.'

JOSEPH CAMPBELL[1]

I was going to start this conclusion by saying something like 'Even by the end of this book we have barely scratched the surface of the shadow...', but when I thought about it, I realized this wasn't actually true. If you have explored what's in your bag, dropped your masks, found the lotuses in your mud, healed your parental shadow, looked into your ancestral past, integrated your sexual story and really engaged with the rest of the practices, then you have definitely more than scratched the surface of the shadow. And yet, as I'm sure you can feel, the shadow is so deep and so dark and so golden and so bright that integrating it fully is a lifetime's work.

So, apart from being sure to *do* the practices in this book, how do we keep Doing the Shadow Work?

I'm going to indulge my 'shameless promotion' shadow here and say that you might like to check out one of my workshops or retreats and/or try my seven-week online 'Embracing the Shadow' course. All the info on these can be found on my website (*see p.232*).

But until then, here are some final thoughts on bringing shadow work into everyday life.

Moving Forward into Darkness

In the Gospel of Thomas, Jesus said, 'What you do not bring forth will destroy you,' which was an invitation to bring our shadows into the light. Buddha, Mohammed, Moses and Jesus all had to face their inner demons, darkness and devils before they could know the glory of godliness. What makes us think that we can avoid what they could not?

The shadow contains aspects that can be potentially harmful to ourselves and others, but 'the destructiveness of the shadow is largely a function of the degree to which we refuse to take responsibility for it'.[2] When we refuse to illuminate our dark side, we are living on dangerous ground, because if we allow it to fester, it will grow more powerful, whereas if we bear loving witness to it, we befriend it and transmute its energy.

The safest and greatest gift we can give the world is an integrated shadow. Over the decade that has passed between the first and second iterations of this book, the world has changed in many huge and sometimes terrifying ways, and never has the time for shadow work been riper than now. Never has there been a better moment to integrate our darkness and own our inner gold. The world needs shadow workers more than ever.

It's been said that the aim of shadow work is not changed behaviour, but changed understanding, out of which a change in behaviour arises.[3] Whether through changed understanding or changed behaviour, writing this book has definitely changed me for the better and I hope that reading it has in some way done the same for you.

Five Tips for Shadow Work in Everyday Life

To help your beneficial change to continue, here are five tips for moving forward on the path of shadow work:

1. Move towards the places that scare you

One of my mentors, the shamanic practitioner Ya'Acov Darling Khan, once asked his Peruvian Achua shaman how to work with his shadow, to which he replied, 'Whatever frightens you, move towards it. Get to know what makes you afraid.'

Within every fear lies a shadow, and within every shadow lies the gold of our innate vitality. Fear is often the sound of the ego resisting the integration of the shadow. We make a comrade out of our shadow every time we go through an initiation of fear. So I ask you, 'What are you scared of in everyday life and how can you explore that fear safely?' Whether it's singing in public, picking up a house spider, going wing-walking if you're not good with heights (as I did recently), facing your fears in everyday life not only integrates the shadow, but also moves you towards fearlessness, which is, of course, not the absence of fear, but the courageous befriending of it.

2. Every day, in every way, embrace your Magnificent Messiness, with love

Shadow work isn't about fixing ourselves (we were never broken in the first place), it's about showing up authentically, and unconditionally loving ourselves and others in all our Magnificent (and very human) Messiness.

3. Be fascinated by projection

Most of us are constantly projecting and most of the time we are totally unaware of this. So much of the harm we do to ourselves and others is based on mistaking our projections for the truth. If we could learn to recognize this, we would become kinder to ourselves and others. This realization can save our relationships.

Every day, every time you are triggered, pause and ask yourself these three questions:

'Am I ever like that?'

'Have I ever been like that in the past?'

'Do I secretly wish I *could* be like that sometimes?'

4. Plant lotus seeds

Lotus flowers cannot grow from polished crystal, they grow from the sometimes foul-smelling soil of the human condition. Shadow work won't protect us from the inevitability of old age, sickness and death, nor will it armour-plate our heart so that it never breaks. But it will allow us to enter these places with more love and more awareness, and perhaps even plant lotus seeds there instead of just wallowing in the mud.

5. Look to your dreams

By opening up to our dreams, we are opening up to the shadow. When we dream, we are a captive audience for the displays of the shadow, so try not to sleep through the show. Simply by remembering, documenting and becoming more conscious of your dreams, you will start to bring your shadow work into your sleep. And if you want to go one step further, then please do check out my books and courses on lucid dreaming.

Owning Our Gold

The mythologist Joseph Campbell famously told his students to *follow their bliss.* Later in life, frustrated by the misinterpretation of his words, he said that he should have told them to follow their *blisters.*

The journey to the mountaintop is an adventure. It is a hero's journey into the golden shadow and we must be prepared for challenges.

Integrating our golden shadow is perhaps the hardest part of all shadow work. The egocentric mind's dominance relies on a constant maintenance of the status quo. It will strive just as hard to keep us away from our golden shadow as it will to deny our dark one. Owning our gold is a direct challenge to its dominance. So, it is far easier to label our blinding inner light as separate from ourselves and project it outside. And with this comes the creation of gods and gurus.

But however powerful, infinite and astonishing the content of our golden shadow, we must try to accept that it is not the power of another being working through us, but our own divine nature calling out to be seen.

Owning our gold will change everything. If we truly accept that the seed of full spiritual awakening is already germinating within us, then how can we possibly go on living the way we have been? Perhaps that's why it's such a threat to our egocentricity?

Suppressing or refusing to befriend the dark shadow may lead to outbursts of anger, jealousy or self-sabotage, but what happens if we refuse to face our golden shadow? Psychologist Abraham Maslow is clear about this. He says, 'If you deliberately plan to be less than you are capable of being, then I warn you that you will be unhappy for the rest of your life.'[4]

So, when it's your time to shine, as it always is, shine fiercely and unapologetically. We are happiest when we are expressing our golden potential. For what is happiness but freely expressing our inner light and rejoicing in the light of others?

Five Tips for Stepping into Your Gold

Here are five tips for continuing to integrate your golden shadow in everyday life:

1. Keep it playful

Some people lose faith in their ability to own their gold by taking the whole thing too seriously and then giving up when they don't step into its full manifestation overnight. To avoid this, if part of your golden shadow is a love of dance, for example, don't sign up for advanced ballet straight away, instead go to an 'ecstatic dance' class where you can release your gold in a playful and safe way. If it's your spiritual gold that you want to integrate, then don't go straight into a 10-day silent Vipassana retreat, but do a regular evening drop-in meditation class to begin with. Keep it playful and take your time.

2. Make friends with your past

The heavy clouds of who we used to be often prevent us from seeing the bright sunlight of our golden potential. When I first started teaching lucid dreaming and shadow work, it was fear that someone with a past like mine (sex, drugs and hip hop) shouldn't be teaching that was the greatest hindrance to stepping into my potential. Now I realize who *better* to be teaching shadow work than someone with a past like that? If you can befriend your past and start to direct your light forward, your golden potential will manifest with far greater ease.

3. Step into your light

I know it's terrifying, but just experiment with it. Bit by bit, start choosing to do things differently. Just small things. Start going to those singing classes you've always dreamed of, start wearing the clothes you actually like, start applying for that job that you've always wanted, and little by little you'll find that you're moving into your light already.

Whenever you're finding it challenging to step into your light or take an opportunity that asks you to shine, maybe you can think: *How would I respond to this situation if I were free of my shadow of fear?* and perhaps even, *If this were all a dream, would I still say 'no'?*

4. Be kind

It's been said that our compassion arises from our very fallibility and that 'love takes root in the soils of human error',[5] so be kind to yourself as you progress on the path and know that everyone else is probably working with similar shadow stuff too.

Every time we are unkind or believe that we are more important than everyone else, we further our separation from love and solidify our shadow content. But the moment that we see others as equally important or even more important than ourselves, we seem to short-circuit the operating system of both the egocentric mind and the shadow that it has created.

5. Share your gold

There is a Buddhist saying: 'When we share our light with others, we do not diminish our own light. Rather, we increase the amount of light available to all.'[6] So, share your gold with others, inspire them to do the same and nurture and encourage those who are yet to see their gold within themselves.

The essence of all of these tips is summed up by this quote from my all-time favourite poet, the 14th-century Persian poet Hafiz:

> 'One regret, dear world,
> That I am determined not to have
> When I am lying on my deathbed
> Is that I did not kiss you enough.'[7]

Last Words

It's been said that 'the essence of bravery is being without self-deception'.[8] Shadow work asks us to wake up and to enter into that bravery, to see ourselves clearly and to accept the shadows of who we are while being open to the true magnificence of who we will become.

Your work with the shadow doesn't stop here and you shouldn't want it to stop here either, because the goal isn't to get rid of the shadow, but to lovingly befriend it and to recognize it as a benevolent force that points you towards your own greatness. By doing so, you not only open up to the possibility of showing love to all aspects of yourself, but also to becoming a more authentic version of yourself, a version that is and always has been a fully awakened being.

Shadow work asks us to 'love the strength and the weaknesses, to love the being lost and the being found, to love the sleep and the awakening'.[9] And it is awakening that this work can lead to. I'm definitely not there yet, and I often find myself stuck in the mud, desperately clutching at lotuses, but I'm closer than before, as you are too, as we Do the Shadow Work together.

So let us wake up and start dreaming our reality into existence, moving into the freedom of shamelessness found in Rumi's field, beyond all notions of darkness and light or wrong and right.

From that place we can love both the brilliance of our divine nature and the Magnificent Messiness of the human condition. We can love it all. For shadow work, as you now know, is all about love.

REFERENCES

Introduction

1. Rumi (1995), 'The Great Wagon', trans. Coleman Banks, *The Essential Rumi*. New York, NY: Quality Paperback Book Club, p.36.

Part I: Meeting the Shadow

1. Hillman, J. (1990), 'The Cure of the Shadow' in *Meeting the Shadow: Hidden power of the dark side of human nature*, eds Connie Zweig and Jeremiah Abram. New York, NY: Jeremy P. Tarcher, p.242.

Chapter 1: What Is the Shadow?

1. Jung, C.G., quoted in Miller, D.P. (1990), 'What the Shadow Knows: An Interview with John A. Sanford' in *Meeting the Shadow: Hidden power of the dark side of human nature*, eds Connie Zweig and Jeremiah Abrams. New York, NY: Jeremy P. Tarcher, p.21.

2. Rob Nairn, in conversation with the author, December 2015.

3. Diamond, S.A., PhD, (2021), 'Essential Secrets of Psychotherapy: What Is the "Shadow"?': www.psychologytoday.com/za/blog/evil-deeds/202101/essential-secrets-of-psychotherapy-what-is-the-shadow [Accessed 1 October 2024]

4. Ya'Acov Darling Khan, in conversation with the author, 2016.

5. von Franz, M-L. (1995), *Shadow and Evil in Fairy Tales*. Originally published in German in three vols; Boulder, CO: Shambhala Publications, Inc.

6. Rilke, R.M. (2001), *Letters to a Young Poet*, trans. Stephen Mitchell. San Francisco, CA: Burning Man Publishing.

7. Johnson, R.A. (1991), *Owning Your Own Shadow*. San Francisco, CA: HarperSanFrancisco.

8. Williamson, M. (2015), *A Return to Love*. Harper Thorsons.

9. David Richo, D. (1999), *Shadow Dance*. Boulder, CO: Shambhala Publications, p.3.

10. Fordham, M. (1978), *Jungian Psychotherapy*. Hoboken, NJ: John Wiley & Sons Ltd, p.5.

11. von Franz, M-L. (2011), Marie-Louise von Franze – "The Shadow": www.youtube.com/watch?v=OvL00iQ0ao4 [Accessed 1 October 2024]

12. Lama Yeshe Rinpoche, www.samyeling.org/quotes/

Chapter 2: Why Do the Shadow Work?

1. Campbell, J. (1989), *The Power of Myth*. New York, NY: Bantam Doubleday Dell, p.120.

2. Villines, Z. (2023), 'What is Shadow Work? What to Know': www.medicalnewstoday.com/articles/what-is-shadow-work [Accessed 1 October 2024]

3. Rob Nairn, in conversation with the author, 2015.

4. Jung, C.G., quoted in Miller, D.P. (1990), 'What the Shadow Knows: An interview with John A. Sanford' in *Meeting the Shadow: Hidden power of the dark side of human nature*, eds Connie Zweig and Jeremiah Abrams. New York, NY: Jeremy P. Tarcher, p.21.

5. Jung, C.G. (1912), 'On the Psychology of the Unconscious' in *Collected Works, Vol. VII: Two Essays on Analytical Psychology*. Princeton, NJ: Princeton University Press, 1992, p.35.

6. Rob Nairn, in conversation with the author, 2015.

Chapter 4: Seeing the Shadow in Others

1. Ben Nachmani, S. (1977), quoted in *Peter's Quotations: Ideas for our time*, ed. Laurence J. Peter, New York, NY: Bantam Books, 1979 edition, p.25.

2. Rob Nairn, in conversation with the author.

3. Richo, D. (1999), *Shadow Dance*. Boulder, CO: Shambhala Publications, p.14.

4. Shaheen, K. (2024), *The Shadow Work Journal*. London: HQ, p.26.

5. Wilbur, K. (1990), 'Taking Responsibility for Your Shadow' in *Meeting the Shadow: Hidden power of the dark side of human nature*, eds Connie Zweig and Jeremiah Abrams. New York, NY: Jeremy P. Tarcher, 1990, p.274.

6. LePera, N. (2024), *Shadow Work Journal*: www.scribd.com/document/704495747/Shadow-Work-Journal [Accessed 1 October 2024]

7. Wilbur, *op. cit.*

8. Professor Geoffrey Lantz, Skype conversation with the author, December 2016.

9. Wood, D., *et al.* (2010), 'Perceiver effects as projective tests: what your perceptions of others say about you', *Journal of Personality and Social Psychology* 99(1), referenced in 'What you say about others says a lot about you, research shows', *ScienceDaily*, August 3, 2010: https://pubmed.ncbi.nlm.nih.gov/20565194/ [Accessed 1 October 2024]

10. Thích Nhất Hạnh, www.goodreads.com/quotes/548044-awareness-is-like-the-sun-when-it-shines-on-things [Accessed 1 October 2024]

Chapter 5: The Childhood Shadow

1. Plato, www.goodreads.com/quotes/19198-we-can-easily-forgive-a-child-who-is-afraid-of [Accessed 1 October 2024]

2. LePera, N. (2024), *Shadow Work Journal*: www.scribd.com/ document/704495747/Shadow-Work-Journal dsf [Accessed 1 October 2024]

3. Brown, B., PhD, (2012), *Daring Greatly*. Sheridan, WY: Gotham Books, p.60.

4. Johnson, R.A. (1991), *Owning Your Own Shadow*. San Francisco, CA: HarperSanFrancisco.

5. Bly, R. (1988), *A Little Book on the Human Shadow*. New York, NY: HarperCollins.

6. Chödrön, P. (2001), *The Places That Scare You*. Boulder, CO: Shambhala Publications; London: HarperElement, 2003, p.113.

Chapter 6: Meeting the Shadow in Dreams

1. Jack Kerouac, www.goodreads.com/quotes/142688-all-human-beings-are-also-dream-beings-dreaming-ties-all [Accessed 1 October 2024]

2. Jung, C.G., quoted in Boa, F. (1988) *The Way of the Dream*. Washington, DC: Windrose Press, p.16.

Part II: Befriending the Shadow

1. Yeats, W.B., www.brainyquote.com/quotes/william_butler_yeats_383082 [Accessed 1 October 2024]

2. Mingyur Rinpoche (2007), *The Joy of Living*, public talk DVD, recorded in Hartford, USA, 9 August.

Chapter 7: Acceptance, Forgiveness and Gratitude

1. Robert Holden, in conversation with the author, October 2016.

2. *Ibid.*

3. *Ibid.*

4. *Ibid.*

5. Brown, J., and Wong, J. (2017), 'How Gratitude Changes You and Your Brain': https://greatergood.berkeley.edu/article/item/how_gratitude_changes_you_and_your_brain [Accessed 1 October 2024]

6. Achor, S. (2011), 'The Happy Secret to Better Work': www.ted.com/talks/shawn_achor_the_happy_secret_to_better_work [Accessed 1 October 2024]

Chapter 8: Understanding the Building Blocks of the Shadow

1. Rob Nairn, in conversation with the author.

2. Brown, B., PhD (2012), *Daring Greatly*. Sheridan, WY: Gotham Books, p.68.

3. Leahy, R., PhD (2016), 'The Gift of Fear: How evolution protected us by making us afraid': www.psychologytoday.com/blog/anxiety-files/201605/the-gift-fear [Accessed 1 October 2024]

4. Neuman, F., MD (2012), 'Easy Phobias to Treat and Hard Phobias': www.psychologytoday.com/blog/fighting-fear/201207/easy-phobias-treat-and-hard-phobias [Accessed 1 October 2024]

Chapter 9: Dropping the Masks That We Wear

1. Rumi: www.goodreads.com/quotes/6849187-tear-off-the-mask-your-face-is-glorious [Accessed 1 October 2024]

2. Cited in Hari, J. (2015), Everything you think you know about addiction is wrong': www.ted.com/talks/johann_hari_everything_you_think_you_know_about_addiction_is_wrong [Accessed 1 October 2024]

3. Kain, E. (2011), 'Ten years after decriminalization drug abuse down by half in Portugal': www.forbes.com/sites/erikkain/2011/07/05/ten-years-after-decriminalization-drug-abuse-down-by-half-in-portugal/#26811fa63001 [Accessed 1 October 2024]

4. Jung, C.G. (1953), *Two Essays on Analytical Psychology*. London: Routledge & Kegan Paul, p.190.

5. Hillman, J. (1990), 'The Cure of the Shadow' in *Meeting the Shadow: Hidden power of the dark side of human nature*, eds Connie Zweig and Jeremiah Abrams. New York, NY: Jeremy P. Tarcher, p.242.

Chapter 10: Befriending the Shadow in Dreams

1. Bly, R. (1988), *A Little Book on the Human Shadow*. New York, NY: HarperCollins, p.49.

2. Preece, R. (2006), *The Psychology of Buddhist Tantra*. Ithaca, NY: Snow Lion Publications; 2012 edition, p.14.

3. Justin Havens, in conversation with the author, August 2016.

4. Zadra, A.L., and Pihl, R.O. (1997), 'Lucid dreaming as a treatment for recurrent nightmares': www.ncbi.nlm.nih.gov/pubmed/8996716 [Accessed 1 October 2024]

5. *Ibid.*

6. Quoted in van den Bout, J. (2006), 'Lucid dreaming treatment for nightmares: a pilot study': https://pubmed.ncbi.nlm.nih.gov/17053341 [Accessed 1 October 2024]

7. Tenzin Wanygal Rinpoche (1998), *Tibetan Yogas of Dream and Sleep*. Ithaca, NY: Snow Lion Publications, p.103.

8. Yount, G., *et al.* (2023), 'Decreased posttraumatic stress disorder symptoms following a lucid dream healing workshop': https://doi.org/10.1037/trm0000456 [Accessed 1 October 2024]

9. *Ibid.*

10. Dr Garret Yount, in conversation with the author, 2024.

Part III: Transmuting the Shadow

1. Johnson, R.A. (1991), *Owning Your Own Shadow*. San Francisco, CA: HarperSanFrancisco, p.17.

Chapter 11: No Mud, No Lotus

1. Thích Nhất Hạnh (2015), *No Mud, No Lotus: The art of transforming suffering*. Ypsilanti, MI: Parallax Press, p.15.

2. Shukman, H. (2014), 'Beautiful Storm: Finding the hidden remedies in our troubled selves': http://tricycle.org/magazine/beautiful-storm [Accessed 1 October 2024]

3. Rendon, J. (2015), 'How Trauma Can Change You—for the Better': http://time.com/3967885/how-trauma-can-change-you-for-the-better [Accessed 1 October 2024]

4. Hefferon, K., *et al.* (2009), 'Post-traumatic growth and life threatening physical illness: a systematic review of the qualitative literature': www.researchgate.net/profile/Kate_Hefferon/publication/23185195_Post-traumatic_growth_and_life_threatening_physical_illness_A_systematic_review_of_the_qualitative_literature/links/543ebd8e0cf21c84f23cb038.pdf [Accessed 1 October 2024]

5. Linda and Charlie Bloom (2016), 'Post Traumatic Growth: The benefits of stress': www.psychologytoday.com/blog/stronger-the-broken-places/201610/post-traumatic-growth [Accessed 1 October 2024]

6. Rendon, *op. cit.*

Chapter 12: Healing the Parental Shadow

1. Ram Dass., www.ramdass.org/ram-dass-quotes/ [Accessed 8 November 2024]

2. Stephen Victor, in conversation with the author, October 2016.

3. Biddulph, S. (1995), *Manhood*. Sydney, NSW: Finch Publishing, p.43.

4. Lama Choyin Rangdrol, in conversation with the author, summer 2015.

5. Whitfield, C.L., MD (1987), *Healing the Child Within: Discovery and recovery for adult children of dysfunctional families*. Deerfield Beach, FL: Health Communications, Inc., p.73.

6. Shaheen, K. (2024), *The Shadow Work Journal*. London: HQ, p.51.

Chapter 13: Integrating the Ancestral Shadow

1. Callanan, L. (2004), *The Cloud Atlas*. New York, NY: Delacorte Press.

2. Dias, B.G., and Ressler, K.J. (2013), 'Parental olfactory experience influences behavior and neural structure in subsequent generations': https://tinyurl.com/yt45f855 [Accessed 1 October 2024]

3. Aoued, H.S., *et al.* (2019), 'Reversing behavioral, neuroanatomical, and germline influences of intergenerational stress': www.biologicalpsychiatryjournal.com/article/S0006-3223(18)31781-5/fulltext [Accessed 1 October 2024]

Chapter 14: Exploring the Sexual Shadow

1. Sergio Magaña, in conversation with the author.

2. Brown, B., PhD (2012), *Daring Greatly*. Sheridan, WY: Gotham Books, p.103.

3. *Ibid.*, p.104

4. Sergio Magaña (2014), *The Toltec Secret*. London: Hay House, pp.84–5.

Chapter 15: Death: The Ultimate Shadow

1. Watts, A., www.azquotes.com/quote/1078453

2. Schimel, J., *et al.* (2007), 'Is death really the worm at the core? Converging evidence that worldview threat increases death-thought accessibility': 789–803: https://doi.org/10.1037/0022-3514.92.5.789 [Accessed 1 October 2024]

3. *Ibid.*

4. Honor Whiteman (2016), 'Athletes' performance improved by thoughts of death': www.medicalnewstoday.com/articles/313836.php [Accessed 1 October 2024]

5. *Ibid.*

6. Check out www.london.samye.org/services/bardo-group for more info.

7. Visit www.deathcafe.com for more info.

8. Dr Angela Halley, 'Embracing Death and Dying' day, Samye Dzong, London, November 2016.

9. Levine, S. (1997), *A Year to Live*. Washington, DC: Bell Tower Publishing, p.69.

Conclusion

1. Campbell, J. (1988), *The Power of Myth*. New York, NY: Doubleday. Quoted in *Joseph Campbell and the Power of Myth* with Bill Moyers (2001), PBS television series, Mystic video.

2. Jung, C.G. (1945), 'The Philosophical Tree', in *Collected Works, Vol. XIII: Alchemical Studies* (1968). London: Routledge & Kegan Paul, p.335.

3. Diamond, S.A., PhD (2021)', 'Essential Secrets of Psychotherapy: What is the "shadow"?': www.psychologytoday.com/blog/evil-deeds/201204/essential-secrets-psychotherapy-what-is-the-shadow [Accessed 1 October 2024]

4. Quoted in Neehall-Davidson, J. (2004), *Perfecting Your Private Practice*. Bloomington, IN: Trafford Publishing, p.95.

5. Low, J. (2006), *Being Guru Rinpoche: A commentary on Nuden Dorje's terma Vidyadhara Guru Sadhana*. Bloomington, IN: Trafford Publishing, p.72, in reference to Tantric practice rather than specifically shadow work.

6. Quoted in Neehall-Davidson, *op. cit.*

7. Quoted in Ladinsky, D. (ed.) (2006), *I Heard God Laughing: Poems of Hope and Joy: Renderings of Hafiz*. London: Penguin Books, reprint edition, p.44.

8. Chödrön, P. (2001), *The Places That Scare You*, Boulder, CO: Shambhala Publications; London: HarperElement, 2003, p.113.

9. Robert Holden, in conversation with the author, summer 2016.

RESOURCES

Here are some of my recommendations for continuing your exploration of the shadow and lucid dreaming.

Shadow Work Books

Lama Tsultrim Allione, *Feeding Your Demons*, Hay House UK, 2009

Steve Biddulph, *Manhood*, Finch Publishing, 1995

Robert Bly, *A Little Book on the Human Shadow*, HarperCollins, 1988

Brené Brown, PhD, *Daring Greatly*, Gotham Books, 2012

Pema Chödrön, *The Places That Scare You*, Shambhala Publications, 2001; HarperElement edition, 2003

Debbie Ford, *The Dark Side of the Light Chasers*, Hodder Paperbacks, 2001

Robert A. Johnson, *Owning Your Own Shadow*, HarperSanFrancisco, 1991

David Richo, *Shadow Dance*, Shambhala Publications, 1999

Keila Shaheen, *The Shadow Work Journal*, HQ, 2024

Connie Zweig and Jeremiah Abrams (eds), *Meeting the Shadow: Hidden power of the dark side of human nature*, a selection of essays by various authors, Jeremy P. Tarcher, 1990

Shadow Workshops and Lucid Dreaming Retreats

I continue to run in-person shadow workshops and lucid dreaming retreats around the world. Come join me for one! See www.charliemorley.com for more information.

I also invite you to connect with me on social media: Charlie Morley Lucid Dreaming.

Shadow Work Online Courses

I have a selection of online courses on both shadow work and lucid dreaming. The details of all of these can be found at www.charliemorley.com.

Death Awareness

Check out the Bardo Group at www.london.samye.org/deathanddying for more info on the volunteers in London who offer practical assistance to those approaching the end of life.

Visit www.deathcafe.com if you want to find out more about talking about death over tea and cake.

ACKNOWLEDGEMENTS

The acknowledgements section from the 2017 edition of *Dreaming Through Darkness* was pages long and the process of thanking people from the eight years between then and now feels overwhelming and impossible. There are simply too many to thank.

My goal with both *Dreaming Through Darkness* and this new iteration has been to introduce people to the powerful healing potential of shadow work, so if you have ever attended one of my shadow work courses or retreats, then I thank you for helping to manifest this goal.

I would also like to express my gratitude to all the people who have helped me write this book and helped me be everything I can be. I take full responsibility for any errors or inaccuracies within the text and I apologize for any and all of these. Huge thanks to my late mum, my dad, my brother Joey, Chloe, Waffles, Bao and my extended family, who have been so supportive over the past few years. To Lama Zangmo and to all the London Samye Dzong *sangha* and to all the Samye Dzong centres at which I have had the privilege of teaching. To my shadow and my dreams. To my teachers Lama Yeshe Rinpoche, Akong Rinpoche, Rob Nairn and Lama Zangmo for their kindness and patience with me.

Thank you to my friends: Mantis Clan, Robbie C, Zia, Dynamic Stag, Donna, Jade, Millie and the Chaotic Pond Otters.

Thank you to Leah for her PR, Vishen and Mindvalley for the amazing new adventures and Awake Academy for the courses.

To Michelle, Jo, Julie, Kezia, Lizzie and the rest of the brilliant team at Hay House for all their hard work.

And finally, thank you for taking the time to read this book. I sincerely hope that it benefits you in some way and that it helps you to integrate your shadow fully and completely for the benefit of all beings.

INDEX

ABOUT THE AUTHOR

Charlie Morley is a bestselling author and teacher of lucid dreaming, shadow integration and Mindfulness of Dream & Sleep. He has been lucid dreaming for over 25 years and was 'authorized to teach' within the Kagyu school of Tibetan Buddhism by Lama Yeshe Rinpoche in 2008. Since then he has written four books, which have been translated into 15 languages, and has run workshops and retreats in more than 20 countries.

He has spoken at both Oxford and Cambridge universities and run courses and given talks for the Metropolitan Police, Reuters News Agency and the Army Air Corps, as well as presenting his work with military veterans on Sky News and at the Ministry of Defence Mindfulness Symposium. In 2018 he was awarded a Winston Churchill Fellowship to research PTSD treatment in military veterans and continues to teach workshops for people with trauma-affected sleep. These teachings form the core of his book *Wake Up to Sleep*.

In 2019, in a world first, he trained a group of therapists to use lucid dreaming with their clients. An expanded and updated 100-hour version of this course ran again in 2023 under the title 'Lucid Dream Facilitator Training'.

In 2023, the first scientific study into Charlie's methods was published in the peer-reviewed journal *Traumatology*, in which 85 per cent of participants experienced 'a remarkable decrease in PTSD symptoms' through using lucid dreaming to transform their nightmares.

Charlie formally became a Buddhist at the age of 19, lived at the Kagyu Samye Dzong London Buddhist centre for seven years and completed a three-month solitary meditation retreat at the Tara Rokpa centre in South Africa in 2016.

He trained and worked as an actor and scriptwriter before running a hip-hop collective called THROWDOWN throughout his twenties. He now lives in London with his partner, Chloe, and their two dogs, Waffles the Wiener and Bao the Chow Chow. When he's not teaching, he enjoys kickboxing, surfing and pretending to meditate.

🌐 charliemorley.com

📷 @charlie_morley_lucid_dreaming

𝐟 @Charlie Morley- Lucid Dreaming

CONNECT WITH
HAY HOUSE
ONLINE

🌐 hayhouse.co.uk   **f** @hayhouse

📷 @hayhouseuk   **X** @hayhouseuk

▶ @hayhouseuk   ♪ @hayhouseuk

Find out all about our latest books & card decks • Be the first
to know about exclusive discounts • Interact with our authors
in live broadcasts • Celebrate the cycle of the seasons with us
• Watch free videos from your favourite authors •
Connect with like-minded souls

*'The gateways to wisdom and knowledge
are always open.'*

Louise Hay